Then...There Was Light

Naomi Ortiz

TRILOGY CHRISTIAN PUBLISHERS
TUSTIN, CA

Trilogy Christian Publishers
A Wholly Owned Subsidiary of Trinity Broadcasting Network
2442 Michelle Drive
Tustin, CA 92780

Copyright © 2020 by Naomi Ortiz

All Scripture quotations, unless otherwise noted, taken from THE HOLY BIBLE, NEW INTERNATIONAL VERSION®, NIV® Copyright © 1973, 1978, 1984, 2011 by Biblica, Inc.® Used by permission. All rights reserved worldwide.

Scripture quotations marked (KJV) taken from The Holy Bible, King James Version. Cambridge Edition: 1769.

All rights reserved, including the right to reproduce this book or portions thereof in any form whatsoever.

For information, address Trilogy Christian Publishing

Rights Department, 2442 Michelle Drive, Tustin, Ca 92780.

Trilogy Christian Publishing/ TBN and colophon are trademarks of Trinity Broadcasting Network.

For information about special discounts for bulk purchases, please contact Trilogy Christian Publishing.

Manufactured in the United States of America

Trilogy Disclaimer: The views and content expressed in this book are those of the author and may not necessarily reflect the views and doctrine of Trilogy Christian Publishing or the Trinity Broadcasting Network.

10 9 8 7 6 5 4 3 2 1

Library of Congress Cataloging-in-Publication Data is available.

ISBN 978-1-64773-139-7

ISBN 978-1-64773-140-3

Contents

Dedication v

Chapter 1. 1

Chapter 2. 35

Chapter 3. 81

Chapter 4. 135

Chapter 5. 181

Chapter 6. 219

References 225

About the Author 231

This book is dedicated to my seven loving children; Ronald, Candace, James, David, Deborah, Thomas, and Marion. Each one is a wonderful blessing from our merciful Savior, Jesus Christ, our Lord.

God's Word says, Isaiah 46:10, "Declaring the end from the beginning, and from ancient times the things that are not yet done, saying, My counsel shall stand, and I will do all my pleasure" (KJV). And that He chose us and planned our lives before time began, as in Psalm 139:13–18.

To every thing there is a season,
And a time for every purpose under heaven:
A time to be born, and a time to die;
A time to plant, and a time to pluck what is planted;
A time to kill, and a time to heal;
A time to break down, and a time to build up;
A time to weep and a time to laugh;
A time to mourn, and a time to dance;
A time to cast away stones, and a time to gather stones;
A time to embrace, and a time to refrain from embracing;
A time to gain, and a time to lose;
A time to keep, and a time to throw away;
A time to tear, and a time to sew;
A time to keep silent, and a time to speak;
A time to love, and a time to hate;
A time of war, and a time of peace.

—(Ecclesiastes 3:1–8 KJV)

CHAPTER 1

Heritage

June 24, 2010

God planned all of our lives, long before time began. He took people from every walk of life all over the earth to make our families who they are today. There is no pure white race. Everyone has ancestors from other races and other cultures locked inside them, which makes them who they are.

Mother's Family

My mother's father came from a Greek island called Cypress. Everyone thought he was from Greece, but he was not. He came over on a boat when he was twenty-one-years old to make his life better. He originally intended to come to America, make a lot of money, and send for the rest of his family back in Cyprus. That never happened. He fell in love with my grandmother, Ruby Kounnas, and had seven children. Just supporting them was enough of an issue, and they settled in Crum Lynne, Pennsylvania. I never had the opportunity to know my father's dad as he died very young at forty-eight.

My oldest relatives were Grampy and Granny Kounnas. Savas Constantine Kounnas and Ruby, as well as my dad's mother, Agnes Radle. They were loving, giving, wonderful people who loved the Lord and as well as everyone else. Granny Radle raised twenty-one children because her oldest daughter, who was my dad's sister, died giving birth to her sixth child. She died in my dad's arms. Granny Radle had fifteen of her own and six of her grandchildren from her daughter. My granny Ruby Kounnas was born and raised in Hershey, Pennsylvania. Her maiden name was Williams. An interesting fact about her was that she never married until she was thirty-two. An interesting fact about my grampy Savas was that on Cypress Island where he grew up, he was a sponge diver. Grampy could hold his breath for longer than five minutes underwater while he was looking for sponges. One day, while he was diving, a storm brewed in the ocean, and he couldn't find the surface and al-

It was always fun for us to visit them when we could. Especially when I went alone, that was the best. I was the oldest grandchild, and my parents allowed me to spend whole summers over their house. Even though my parents and siblings lived so close to them, I could walk home when I wanted to, but I chose to stay as long as possible.

Every afternoon we played 500 Rummy, just for fun. My grampy and granny played cards with me many times that I stayed over with them. Grampy also made homemade wines out of many things he grew, like grapes, blackberries, and even dandelion wine. He had a root cellar that had a dirt floor where he stored his wine. He also smoked cigars but only when he drank with his friend, George.

Father's Family

My dad's mother's maiden name was Agnes Hollandback. She was born and raised in Moosic, PA, where she lived her whole life, as well as died there. Moosic is close to Scranton in the Pocono Mountains.

My dad's father, George Washington Radle, was born and raised in South Dakota. He was a carpenter by trade. George had one sister named Dora, and she came to Moosic and married a Tucker, who was Russell

Tucker's brother, Russell married Aunt Sharlotte, who was dad's sister.

Dad's family all knew the Lord Jesus Christ as well, and all were kind and loving people. Granny Radle had fourteen kids with George Washington Radle, and Dora had seven and died giving birth to her seventh child. This is how Granny Radle had the opportunity to raise all twenty-one children. I will never know how, but she fed and clothed all those kids. That is how my father was raised in such a large family. They had a large oval table where ten of them could eat at a time, then the other eleven sat down and ate out of the same plates. My mom even ate with them while she was dating my dad. How they survived and had enough income was amazing. Everyone worked and gave all their money to Granny. She used to give my dad $.50 to take my mom to the movies.

July 10, 2010

I just came out of surgery for breast cancer yesterday, and thanks be to God again for carrying me through it. He always does over, and above all, I can think, or man can do. The breast cancer is gone, and once again, I am free. God is so loving and kind; He is faithful and patient with us. I don't even have any pain, and I know that is my Lord's doing. I also know He carried me through this surgery and my last three hernia surgeries with no pain too. Human words cannot express the goodness of our God.

I could write another book about the values, philosophy, and religious beliefs of my dad's family, and hopefully, all of the characteristics I've inherited have come from my heavenly Father and not necessarily from Dad's line. Our heritage is a golden one, of a long line of Christians who genuinely lived for and loved the Lord our God. Way, way back, we have grandparents and great grandparents who worshiped the Lord and were born-again saints of God. Some were Baptist, some were Pentecostal, and some were Methodists. No matter what they called themselves, they loved the Lord and lived clean, good lives. Their values were taken from God's Word, the Bible. None of them were perfect, but they were saved.

My dad's father was a machinist and a carpenter. I think for a short time, he worked with Grampy Kounnas at Baldwin's Locomotive making trains. My dad's mother, as far as I knew, never worked outside the home. Her work was home caring for twenty-one children, a huge house, and family needs. She worked though; you can bet on that!

July 12, 2010

I don't have much more to say about my dad's family, but I would like to say, praise the Lord! For He is good! His mercies are new every morning, and they endure through all generations (Lamentations 3:23; Psalm 100:5).

July 24, 2010

I woke up at 6:00 a.m. to hear a message from my son Ronald. He and Bethany were at the Lowes Cinema in Cherry Hill, NJ, when four men tried to hi-jack them and their Jeep. Praise God! They locked their doors and got away. We are definitely in the end times because my granddaughter Natalie's baby drowned in my daughter Deborah's pool, and Deborah revived him using CPR. Glory to God! And Angel's son swallowed a quarter, which lodged in his throat, but he was also saved. We are the heritage of the mighty God, and He cares for His own.

My mother shared many stories with me about her own parent's childhood. One story she told us was that Grampy Kounnas (Savas) was born in Cyprus, a Greek island, and how he worked diving for sponges in the sea, which I have already mentioned. Mom also told about

Granny Kounnas and how she favored Joy, my sister, because her middle name was the same as her "Ruby". Every time she came to our house, she had something for Joy, which broke my heart. I was too little to understand why she favored Joy. I don't know too much about their childhood, except that they once lived in Atlantic City, before the casinos.

My mom's maiden name was Kounnas. She was born on September 29, 1923, in Chester, PA, but she grew up in Atlantic City. They moved to Crum Lynne, PA, because the jobs were scarce in Atlantic City, and my grampy had gone to work at Baldwin's, as I mentioned. She used to tell us a lot of stories about her childhood. One was when Grampy, her dad, caught her smoking. To punish her, he made her sit down and smoke a whole cigar. After she finished, she got so sick she never smoked again. Another story was when she and her friend ate some rock salt at a carnival and got awful sick.

Once she told us a story about some friends and herself went into a man's garden to steal pumpkins on Halloween, and she got caught, but her friends got away. Of course, she tells us it wasn't her fault because she was the youngest. Her dad gave her an awful spanking. Grampy had an actual woodshed, where he took his kids, and my mom to give them a spanking when they were bad. She keeps telling us a story of having terrible eczema, which is a bad skin irritation. She said Grampy took her to the clinic on the boardwalk in Atlantic City, where they lanced her neck and got a cup of puss out, so she says, and they didn't even give her an aspirin.

She also told us that where they lived was in an apartment and the man downstairs played the bagpipes. My mom was scared to death of him. A lady in the same apartment building always took all the cream off the milk because, in those days, the milkman delivered milk to your doorstep.

Mom in My Childhood

Mom was the only disciplinarian in the house. She must have gotten tired of disciplining after me because no one else ever received any discipline. I did chores like cleaning the bathroom, doing the dishes, washing the kitchen floor, cooking, and taking care of the babies. No one else ever did anything. When I spoke up and complained, she would smack me in the mouth.

A happy memory I have of my mom is her always being there and cooking good food and baking homemade bread and pies. But the best thing she ever did was take us to Sunday School. We also went to Bible School in the summer when school let out. It is because of her that I have lots of Word in my heart, which the Holy Spirit uses when someone needs help.

A painful memory of my mom was how she always accused me of being a whore, and I wasn't. She would beat me with my dad's belt till I had welts on my arms, legs, and face. Back in those days, child abuse wasn't heard of. You could do almost anything to your kid, and no one cared. I even went to Pastor Bob when I was fourteen or fifteen years old, and he said, "I deserved it." Mom also told everyone in the family that I was bad. So, as a result, my granny left stuff in her will to everyone except me, which hurt me terribly because I loved her. My mom, to this day, does not remember the beatings she gave me, but I know why. I was my dad's favorite, and she was jealous.

July 29, 2010

More important than anything else is the works of Christ Jesus in our family. My husband and I just came home from visiting Ronald and Bethany. We wanted to see them and the kids before going to Virginia Beach tomorrow. Ronald and Linda, Bethany's mom, went to the laundromat when we arrived only Bethany and David, Bethany's dad, and the kids were home. We sat and talked and waited for Ronald to return, when he came home, he told us how God spoke to his heart again. He said it was just like the first time God spoke to him at Lowe's Cinema, except this time it was about a lady who was there in the laundromat. God told Ronald that He wanted to heal her of Multiple Sclerosis (MS) and for Ronald to pray with her. While he was washing his clothes, Linda was talking to the same lady who confided in her that she had MS. The lady also stated she was not in a local church. The Holy Spirit told Ronald that they left their church because of an altercation or problem with the pastor. Ronald was to tell the husband not to look to a pastor, he is just like us, imperfect, but to look to God. Then they prayed with the lady for her to be healed. I am sure that God healed her. He is really pouring out His Spirit on anyone who will listen and obey. We are definitely in the end times, and I praise the Lord for His mercy and faithfulness. His love and goodness are perfect, and His hedge of fire around us keeps us. God is good all the time. God is love, and His love never fails.

I went to an oncologist today. He wants me to start a weeks' worth of radiation on my right breast. I waited and listened, then I said "no" to the Dr. I believe in my heart that God healed me, with the help of my surgeon and that radiation will only hurt me more in the long run. I know God put doctors on this earth to help us, but I also know they are human, like me, and not always 100% right. God uses them, but man has shortcomings and failures, so medicine and man-made things for cures are not always right. If I'm wrong, I apologize to my kids and my husband, but especially to my Lord and Savior. I want to hear from Him and what He wants me to do in all things.

I know God wants me and my family to live long and prosper because His Word tells me so, Romans 8:28. Wonderful is my Redeemer, praise His name. The joy of the Lord is my strength. Never lose your joy. Sometimes you may be sad or unhappy but never lose your joy.

August 11, 2010

I need and want to talk about how my Lord and Savior, Jesus Christ, just blessed us again. We just got home Monday the ninth of August from three beaches. The vacation was our best yet, thanks to our Lord. Isaac kept us at his home for three days in Virginia Beach. Then Billy rented a luxury room in the Hilton Hotel right on the beachfront for $500 per night. It was so beautiful! I don't know how anyone can look out at the endless ocean and the beautiful sunset and think there is no God. I would think they were insane. Then we checked out and came home for one day before we left the next day for Ocean City. We stayed at a Scarborough Inn for two days, then to Cape May for two more days of stay where Ronald and Bethany renewed their wedding vows. What a wonderful vacation, praise the Lord!

God made everything perfect for Ronald, and Bethany, and us as he always does. I had a bucket list, which is everything you desire to do in your heart before you "kick the bucket". Many of them were fulfilled by our stay at the three beaches. I always wanted a professional massage, and we both got one for $100 each. Well worth the price. I've always wanted a large piece of amethyst rock, which I was able to purchase. I always wanted to go to a restaurant where everything was a fondue,' and we did that as well. God knew all the desires of Billy's and my hearts; He is such a good Father.

Danny and Candy were also able to go with us because God supplied extra money to help them for the trip. The best thing He did was cause them to get lost in Wild-Wood. Their brakes actually broke on Danny's car, and they were right in front of an auto body shop that happened to be open on Sundays. They fixed the car for Danny, and the price was reasonable. If they hadn't got lost, they would have been on the A.C. Expressway when the brakes broke, and it could have been a horrible nightmare. God is always so good.

New subject. Savannah fell down the upstairs steps last night and was not hurt! Praise the Lord for He is good. His mercies endure through all generations (Psalm 100:5).

September 4, 2010

I haven't felt like writing much, because my mom is always mad at me for something I never did. I talked to Joy, my sister, last night, and found out why. She told me that Holly, my baby sister, told her that I said mom was ugly, and this book was all about how awful she was. So now I know that is not true.

To talk about my mother's spiritual or religious beliefs alone, my mother would always drag us to Sunday School and church even when we didn't want to go. Then Bible School on top of that in the summertime. I praise God that she did now, because of her, I have a wonderful relationship with Jesus Christ. I wouldn't trade that for all the gold or anything.

My mother is still alive as I write this. She will probably live to be at least 100 years old anyway. Her anger and bitterness are keeping her alive. She is angry at everyone, including my dad and me. He has been dead for quite a while, at least ten years now. She talks about him like he was garbage. My dad wasn't perfect, but he never left her or us. He never cheated or drank or smoked anything while alive as far as I can remember. He usually worked about three jobs to support us. We never had to move because the jobs he worked were enough to pay for our home in Woodlyn. My mom never worked, but she worked hard to raise us kids and keep our home nice.

The most important thing I learned from my mom was understanding Jesus Christ, that He is Lord, and should be Lord of everything in my life. No one or nothing should come before Him. I also learned that this life is just a breath or whisper (the Bible says "a vapor"), and we will spend eternity with God if we give Him our hearts and our lives. We can be saved and baptized and live for Him, and the Bible, the Word of God, is very clear about that. You can't just be saved. You have to be baptized and have a relationship with Jesus. Just like your closest friend. You have to forgive people for hurting you, or Jesus will not forgive you for the sins you have committed. My mom taught me a lot about God's Word, but she never lived it herself, and that is just between her and God.

Believe it or not, there are a lot of good things I remember about my mom, not just bad. If anyone came in while we were eating, she would give them half of her food on the plate. She always cooked wonderful meals for us. I never remember going hungry. We always had clean clothes, and she taught me how to pray. She was very good to her mother and dad. She kept Granny for a few years before she moved in with Uncle James, just before she died.

My dad never told us any stories about his childhood. Anything we were told or learned, came from my mother. For many generations back, we were blessed of God because all my grandparents and great-grandparents loved the Lord. The blessings or heritage of the Lord fell upon us because Gods' word says everything we do and say in our life can either cause a blessing or a cursing. It depends on our ancestors and us. Thank God all of them loved the Lord.

The Names of God:
 Emmanuel—means God with us. "I AM."
 Jehovah—means I AM the One who is the self-existent One.
 El Shaddai—means the all-sufficient One, God Almighty.
 Adonai—means the Lord, my great Lord.
 EL—the strong One.
 El Elohim Yisrael—God the God of Israel.
 El Elyon—the God most high.
 Elohim—the All-Powerful One—Creator.

Elohim—the Eternal God—the Everlasting God.
El Roi—the God who sees me.
Jehovah-Jireh—the Lord will provide.
Jehovah-Mckaddishkem—the Lord who sanctifies.
Jehovah-Nissi—the Lord is my Banner.
Jehovah-Rapha—the Lord who heals.
Jehovah-Rohi—the Lord is my Shepherd.
Jehovah-Sabaoth—the Lord of Hosts, the Lord of Armies.
Jehovah-Shalom—the Lord is peace.
Jehovah-Shammah—the Lord is there... the Lord is my companion.
Jehovah-Tsidkenu—the Lord our Righteousness.
Yahweh—"I AM" the One who is the self-existent One.

No, I didn't make a mistake; the last two names mean the same thing. There are twenty-one in total names for God. Possibly more, we haven't found yet. I thought this was more important than answers about my earthly family, so I will give answers about my Heavenly Father.

September 22, 2010

Just had to write early this morning about all God's recent blessings. He is such a good Father. It's like

Christmas every day with Him. I needed a pair of black shoes to sing in our choir, and of course, I didn't have any. They needed not only to look nice, but they had to be comfortable. Well, I went to many yard sales on Saturday, praying that God would find a pair for me that I could afford without having to go to a store. I was finished with all the sales and on my way home when I noticed a sign for another sale. I went there and right there, in front of me were the shoes. Still in the original shoe box, perfectly in my size, black and so very comfortable. They were Easy Spirit and only $3.00. Ha-ha, God is so good! Even the name is kind of a double meaning. Easy Spirit—God's Holy Spirit, I think that is what they call an Oxymoron. Oh well, it was no coincidence.

I have another story of God's goodness. God definitely has a sense of humor. I woke up one morning about a week ago, earlier than usual, wishing I could sleep later. The people upstairs were up and making noises. I thought to myself, the man upstairs is probably waking me up, another oxymoron. Then I realized that it was God's intention, and He was being the man upstairs to wake me up early to pray.

The funniest thing I ever saw was here at my apartment. I was leaving to run some errands when I went around the corner and noticed a squirrel lying flat on the corner of the step. His arms and legs were hanging over the corner, and his head was down on the side of the steps. He looked like he was dead and flattened by a car. As soon as he saw me, he hopped up and scampered up the tree. I couldn't stop laughing and wished I had had a video camera at that moment.

October 14, 2010

    God is so good, and He is constant and always on time. Candy has an upper respiratory infection and feels miserable. On top of that, she can't see her doctor for three days, and everyone else is sick. Only one antibiotic helps her, and it is Levaquin, which costs $50 because her insurance is so lousy. She doesn't have the money, and I don't either. To make a long story short, God came through again. He never fails us. The lady at CVS Pharmacy went to the window with her pills and said $25. That is half of what they usually cost. Candy asked the lady how she was able to do that. The lady said that CVS gets tons of coupons in for things like Levaquin for people who don't have deductibles on their insurance. That is news to us. But God knew. Without her even asking, God put it on the employees' heart to bless Candy. Isn't He wonderful?
    Psalm 16:11 (NKJV), "…in Your presence is fullness of joy." Amen!

God is love, and love never fails. I named my large purple amethyst "Ebenezer" because "thus far the Lord has helped us" (1 Samuel 7:12 KJV), the meaning of that name.

Dad's sister, Aunt Lil, just died. She was my cousin June's mom. She was ninety-two. Praise the Lord.

Last month God blessed us with newer living room furniture, which Ronald, my son, put on his Ronald and Flanagan charge. While the salesman was talking, Ronald suggested I get the couch I had seen cheaper in Woodlyn at their close-out store. The salesman left to talk to the manager. When he came back, he informed us that the pieces I choose were discontinued items, and no more were in the warehouse. So, we had to pick them up, but instead of paying $2,200.00 for both, we could have them for $890.00. That was a true blessing! Not only did we get the furniture for less than half off, but we got a free HD camcorder. Isn't God wonderful! He does better, over and above anything we can think or do. I love you, Lord, and thank you for all your marvelous blessings, especially my salvation and my kids', Candy, Ronald, Jim, Deborah, Tom, David, and Marion. Thank you for my grandbabies too. They are such a wonderful blessing, Caitlyn, Isaac, Savannah, Alexis, Jayden, Timmy Jr., and Jonathan, Angel, Natalie, Frankie, Bobby, Kaitlyn, Christopher, Casey, Cheyanne,

Lisa, David, Mallory, Brittany, and Brianna, twenty total. Even though I hardly ever see them, they are in my prayers.

Recently I was stopped by a Willingboro Police officer for speeding. He said I was changing lanes without signaling, and I cut some guy off. I was speeding and changed lanes often without using my turn signal. Reminds me of when Jim Carey got stopped and also had a glove box filled with tickets. I was just coming home from Bible Study.

I told him I had to go to the bathroom, and that I was an old lady.

Then he said, "You don't have your seat belt on either."

I said, "Yes, I do. But the shoulder strap is behind me because I had breast cancer, and it hurts me to have it go around the front." I showed him my scar. After that, he "lost it" and turned off his flashlight and handed it to me.

I said, "I think that is yours."

He said, "Oh yeah."

Then he told me to go home, and he would drop my ticket by the next a.m. just for no seat belt because he wanted to give me a break.

I said, "Thank you," and left.

He never came to our home, but a few days later he called me and told me that he was not going to give me a ticket at all. Just a warning. What a Savior! He blessed me again at this time. I definitely didn't deserve it. But really, when do we ever deserve anything God does? He does it out of His love for us, not because we are good.

Recently I went to Candy's Shop-Rite to shop and was standing in line to check out when the checker and I started talking. Somehow my age came up, and she said, "You're not sixty-three years old, you look forty."

I said, "Thank you very much."

She even called one other cashier to guess my age. I was a little embarrassed that she was making such a big deal out of it. But after I calmed down and my head stopped swelling, I gave all the glory to God for "restoring my youth" like the eagles. He keeps me young inside and out.

November 3, 2010

We took Ginny to a Christmas Tree lighting in Moorestown. It was freezing. She gave us $60.00 for gas and treated us to "Friendly's" for dinner. God is truly wonderful to send us someone like Ginny. She is not only my friend and prayer partner but sometimes, I think she is an angel. She feels the same way about me. When God takes her home, I'm going to be lost. I'm sure He will send me someone else.

November 4, 2010

It's 6:36 a.m., and I am up writing. To see one more sunrise and one more rainbow, the orange, red, and yellow of the beautiful fall trees and my grandbabies smiles are all of God's wonders, and it's more than any of us deserve, especially me. I am so very thankful for this new day, and all the blessings my faithful God bestowed on me. I see Jesus in the faces of all my grandbabies, and He is so beautiful. I don't ever take for granted all the blessings of God. When you are down, and the devil is trying his best to depress you, make a list of all God's blessings. You will find every time that God's blessings far exceed the problem of this life. So far, to date, I have had fourteen operations, including the big "C" cancer, and God has been in everyone and delivered me from everyone. I have had four husbands, seven children, twenty grandchildren, and thirteen great-grandchildren, and not once has God ever let me down. It was during the worst times that He carried me in His arms. Just like in the poem called *Footprints*.

New York Trip

About three weeks ago in October, I bought two tickets for the Dr. Oz show. So, I asked my sister Holly to go with me, which was another one of God's miracles. For me to be able to forgive Holly from stealing my mom's money was not something I was able to do, and also to keep loving her as my sister was just as difficult. God made a way for me to just give it all to Him. If I start to think about it again, the Word says to "take every thought captive" to the obedience of God's Word (2 Corinthians 10:5 NIV). So, I do. It's amazing! Anyway, back to the Dr. Oz show story. It happened to fall on a Wednesday, 10-20-10. The night before was my choir practice at Lighthouse Tabernacle Church. Coming down the steps after practicing my right knee went out, and I was in horrible pain. I could barely walk. I couldn't even get in my V.W. I began to drive home before I realized the steering wheel was higher up. I was afraid to drive home. So, of course, I prayed. When I arrived home, it took all the strength I had to walk from the car to our front door. Finally, inside I thanked God and called Holly to give the bad news about not being able to walk. Therefore, our trip to New York had to be canceled. I also told her that I thought maybe it was a sign from God that we should not go because of something worse that could happen. Then I talked to Deborah, of all the people to set me straight, she said: "Maybe it's not God, maybe it's the devil trying to keep you home because God wants to bless you." So, I put icy hot on my knee and rubbed it and laid hands on it, and claimed God's word over myself. In the end chapter of Mark, the Word says,

> *And these signs shall follow them that believe; In My name shall they cast out devils; they shall speak with new tongues; they shall take up serpents; and if they drink any deadly thing, it shall not hurt them; and they shall lay hands on the sick, and they SHALL recover.*
>
> (Mark 16:17–18 KJV)

So, I did, and God healed me by 11:00 p.m. Tuesday night! I called Holly at 7 a.m. on Wednesday and said, "Get ready; we are going to New York!" By the way, not only was all the pain gone, but there was not even any stiffness. To make a long story even longer, we took three trains; The River Line, the Big Train to Penn Station, and then the E Train in the subway to get to 54th Street in New York. But we arrived there early and bought our tickets for Dr. Oz and even had time to eat lunch in the NBC building, where there are tons of stores and small cafes. We ate in one that had the best soup and sandwich I ever had, which was another blessing. The sandwich was on homemade oat bread, with white chicken breast meat and whole slices of avocado, my favorite. The soup was Greek eggplant soup with squash and tomatoes in it. Best soup I have ever tasted.

After lunch, we went to the show to get into line. It was a good thing I had my collapsible chair. We waited and waited and waited. One woman had to be taken out to rest. We waited so long. Finally, we made it in the show. The first announcement that Dr. Oz made was that today, October 20, 2010, was going to be the only day in the whole history of his show that he was giving away $1,000.00 in gifts to every audience member in the room. Holly and I looked at each other, and our chins fell to the floor. No wonder the devil didn't want us there. But God had other plans to bless us. What an amazing, wonderful God we serve. The prizes included a whole year gym membership at twenty-four-hour fitness, which was worth $600.00, as well as a $50.00 Target gift card—my favorite. There was also a $159.00 pair of sketchers sneakers, a one-night stay at the Holiday Inn anywhere in the world, a few of Dr. Oz's favorite vitamins with Omega 3, and fish oil. All that totaled a thousand dollars, he mentioned. Holly and I didn't' take the gym membership because we had to pay a 28% tax on the total in January, which would have been $280.00. We left that and took home all our other gifts. What a blessing! Just spending the day with my sister was a blessing in itself. Also, on the way back to the train we got a bicycle surrey ride from a young black man who was so funny, we couldn't stop laughing. We ate dinner that evening at Roy Rogers, which was nowhere else except in New York. We took two trains home, and all went well. We even talked to a Chinese lady that commuted every day from NJ to NY to work and told us that this day was the only day that the train didn't break down or have to be delayed. What a marvelous God we serve. Isn't He wonderful?

From Stephens Ministry Class

November 17, 2010

NAOMI—Boldness in presenting the gospel and expressing your faith and belief in God with such joy and confidence no matter what the situation. It is evident that you are not ashamed of the gospel of Jesus Christ and love to share it with others whenever the opportunity presents itself. Your bubbly attitude is catching and truly reflects, I believe, what and how God's children should present ourselves to the world and with each other. Continue to let the joy of the Lord be your strength, and through the power of prayer, be steadfast in offering this new life to others whenever you can (Angie Williams 2010–my friend who wrote this about me).

November 27, 2010

I had to back up to last month to write about a special praise report that I didn't have time to write then. Actually, it was an answer to prayer. Brian is a young man who is always at Phil and Delore's house. He is a DJ by trade, and every time we have a Bible Fellowship group at their house, I can tell my spirit that he wants to receive Jesus as His Savior, but something is holding him back from it. I finally found out what it was. Phil was counseling him and telling him that he has to give up everything to come to Christ, even his DJ job. So, I asked Jesus if He would make time, just a few minutes, for me to talk to him and to let him know what the Bible says about that. Jesus said we can come to Him in our sin. That is why He died on Calvary so that we could be justified. Just as if I'd never sinned. God made a way for me to have three minutes alone with him. I told him, "Jesus wants you to know, you can come to Him, just the way you are today, and you don't have to give up anything." His face lit up, and he said, "Thank you, I really needed to know that." There is a wonderful old song called *Just as I Am*. The first verse is "just as I am, without one plea, but that thy blood was shed for me." Praise God, our wonderful heavenly Father.

> *Only one life will soon be past, only what's done for Christ will last.*
> ("Quote by C.T. Studd " n.d.)

Childhood Neighborhood

The place I grew up was the perfect place to raise a child. It was a dead-end street, 1710 Grant Avenue, Woodlyn, PA. There were woods and a bubbling creek, which made a perfect place for me to play. I was a tomboy. I would climb a mulberry tree every morning for fresh berries to go with my cereal. After that, I would go next door to get my best friend, Andrea. We would cross the creek on large stones that were above the water and play in the woods. We even built a treehouse up in a tree. We dammed in part of the creek to make a pool so we could swim. We even pulled bloodsuckers, also known as leaches, off our skin after swimming and flushed them down the toilet.

One day Andrea fell all the way down the bank that led from the road to the woods. There were large stone steps that led all the way from the road down to the woods. They were covered with poison oak. She hit each step and had poison oak all over her whole body. Another time, a pregnant mother opossum got hit by a car and crawled down the bank and died in the woods. Andrea and I got a shoebox and put all her babies in it, there were eight, and fed them with one of her dolly's bottles. Most of them lived. When they were big enough, we released them into the woods. I used to look under large rocks to find small black salamanders to play with.

I also played with large, green praying mantis'. I collected bird feathers. The woods were a bird sanctuary I had one of every bird feather you could imagine. Bluebird, Oriole (yellow), cardinal (red), robin, and even a pheasant and an eagle. I had them mounted and labeled in a scrapbook. One day I came home from school, and my mom had thrown them away. I cried for days. I asked her why, and she replied, "They were full of bugs." We also played in the warm rain. It was clean then. You could even eat the snow as long as it wasn't yellow. Every morning on my way to school, by the way, I walked to school, I would stop at a natural spring by my house and get down on my knees and drink the fresh cold water from the ground. It was icy cold and very refreshing. One day it just dried up.

Jesus said, "Study to show thyself approved unto God, a workman that needeth not to be ashamed, rightly dividing the word of truth" (2 Timothy 2:15 KJV).

Sometimes I think that is why our generation was healthier and lived longer—because the water and the air were clean. There were no dyes or food additives. Everything was natural, and we ate at home almost always. I ate wild strawberries that grew in the grass and mulberries from the tree and blackberries from a vine and tomatoes from Grampy's garden. The whole honeycomb from my dad's honeybees was delicious. All those good things made us healthy and live longer. Don't forget the spring water from the ground. It's a shame our kids can't have the life I had growing up. It was wonderful until I became a teenager.

December 21, 2010

I wish I had the time and the energy to write in this book every day. But each day goes by like a whirlwind. Just like God's word says, our life is a vapor (James 4:14). Here only for a breath, then gone. Praise the Lord, for He is good. His mercies do last through all generations. Yesterday I received the reports from both my doctors.

The sore on my left breast is just a bacterial infection. Glory to God. Also, I spend the whole day with my son Ronald and Isaac and the twins. It was a glorious, beautiful day. Thank you, Jesus. I love you, Lord, because you first loved me.

God has brought me through many valleys and many deep waters. But not once has He allowed them to take me under or any fires to consume me. He has always made a way of escape. Let me name several that God in His infinite mercy has brought me out of. The jungle of Haiti—having a deadly parasite when I got home. My left eye was blinded, and I could not see. My right eye had the vitreous separated. I had two tubal ligations; after the first one, my last son Ronald was born. I had a cyst on my ovary that was bleeding, and the doctors removed that ovary and my appendix. I had three hernia operations. One lithotripsy (kidney stone) I recovered from breast cancer. I had three babies and three miscarriages, one broken collar bone, one broken right arm in fourth grade. I learned to write with my left hand. God delivered me out of them all. Scripture says, "Many are the afflictions of the righteous, but God delivers him out of them all" (Psalm 34:19 KJV).

Another wonderful word is with every temptation, God will make a way of escape (1 Corinthians 10:13). I just wanted to throw that in because we used it Friday night at the Overcomers Meeting. Thank you, Father God, for everything we go through and that You have made a help and a scripture for us to use in the battle. Thank you for my angel. I can feel him when I pray. I love you.

CHAPTER 2

January 1, 2011

Psalms 147:16 (NKJV), "He gives snow like wool; He scatters the frost like ashes."

One of the most beautiful creations our heavenly Father created, besides children, is snow. We had our first snowfall last week—almost two feet. God's blanket of white looked so lovely, and just enough that no one was stranded. I could fill this whole book with our Lord's beautiful blessings. His Word is number one!

Psalms 30:5 (NKJV) "...Weeping may endure for a night, but JOY comes with the morning." Praise God for He is good. Also, "Come unto ME all ye that labor and are heavy laden and I will give you rest" (Matthew 11:28–29 KJV). This is written on the pages of my heart.

Last Friday night Ronald and Billy went with me to Mike's Overcomers' class in our church. I was awarded a nineteen-year coin for being an overcomer. It has XIX on it. Roman numeral for nineteen. I give all the glory to God that I was never addicted to drugs or alcohol, and He delivered me from a personal addiction in 1991, which only God and a few other people know about. But if it weren't for God working in my life, I probably would have been dead by now. He saved me from me a million times and carried me even when I thought He wasn't there. "...All things work together for good, to those who love God" (Romans 8:28 NKJV).

We just had Christmas last week, and every year it gets better and better. But I wish I would have remembered to make a birthday cake for Jesus. Except we are getting so fat, I don't know who would have eaten it. I've wanted a Isaac's Ark clock for about fifteen years, and Holly got me one for Christmas. I really love it. And my yellow V.W. has been chipping paint off the doors and fenders. The company is painting it for free and even gave us a rental van to use. Glory to God! He always gives us favor.

It is almost midnight, and Billy's last day of vacation was today. I better get to bed because tomorrow the alarm clock is going to go off at 5:30 or 6:00 a.m.

January 24, 2011

Deuteronomy 30:19 (NKJV), "...I have set before you life and death, blessing and cursing; therefore choose life, that both you and your descendants may live."

Choosing life in every situation is like the bracelet, What Would Jesus Do, THAT everyone used to wear. When we choose death or sin, it's like the crowd that yelled: "...Give us Barabbas!..." (John 18:40 NIV).

How Important Was Religion Growing Up?

Very important, my mom took us to Sunday school and church every Sunday and Wednesday night prayer meeting. Then when school let out for the summer, she sent us to Daily Vacation Bible school. Thank God for my mother. The Holy Spirit brings up a well spring of Bible verses when I need them for others and for myself. "Thy word that is hid in my heart, that I might not sin against thee" (Psalm 119:11 KJV). Precious word of God. More powerful than any two-edged sword. God spoke and created the heavens and the earth and all that you survey and the Universe with His spoken word. That is why it is so powerful. "thy word is a lamp unto my feet and a light unto my path" (KJV).

February 1, 2011

Praise God, for He is good. I need to find heavenly words in my heart, instead of just thank you. Today I had a CT scan in the hospital for abdominal pain. It showed that the kidney stone I had in my right kidney was "gone". God is more than good and so much more than worthy. He deserves praise and obedience every waking moment we are alive, for all He has done for us. "Greater love hath no man than this, that a man lay down His life for his friends" (John 15:13 KJV). Thank you seems so little to say, so take my life, all I have left, and use me for your purpose.

Most of our social activities were combined with our religious beliefs. All my friends were part of our church, and when I became a teen, we had Pioneer Girls, like girl scouts, but it was in our church. Saturday nights would be our Youth for Christ night. I had no social activities outside of the church. I was not allowed to go to any dances or even my prom. The life my parents choose for us paid off big time. Now I wouldn't know where I would be if it weren't for Jesus Christ. Probably dead a long time ago.

Every Christian religious holiday was celebrated in our home. We never had much, but we always celebrated Christmas and always had a tree. Usually, we all got one gift. For Easter somehow, someway, God always provided Easter dresses for us to wear to church. Mom and Dad had an Easter basket for us when we woke up. WE all knew that there was no bunny—only Jesus who rose from the grave. As for Christmas, I still believe in Santa Clause, and I'm sure that my father God doesn't mind at all. We were even allowed to dress up for Halloween because no one knew then what it stood for. It was totally different when I was a child than it is nowadays. Our neighbors had to guess who we were, or we didn't get any Candy.

I don't remember any health epidemics as a child except the natural childhood diseases like measles, mumps, and chickenpox. We all had them. We were also vaccinated, so we would never get polio.

God's word says, "Many are the afflictions of the righteous, but the LORD delivers him out of them all" (Psalms 34:19 NKJV).

I was never seriously ill as a child. God protected us because, for generations back, we all were saved, born-again Christians who love the Lord. We always had favor with God. But we did have all the childhood diseases, as I mentioned before.

I had one serious accident as a child. My mom told me not to play on a tree that had fallen from a hurricane that we had. I did exactly what she told me not to do, and I fell off and broke my right arm. My hand was hanging on my arm with just a little bit of skin. I was in a cast for six weeks and had to learn to write with my left hand because I was still in school in the fourth grade when it happened.

I don't remember having any fears even till I became a teenager. Then I feared my mother would kill me. She seemed to hate me after I grew up, but I guess she did the best she knew how. Before that, I had the most wonderful childhood anyone could ever have. Nothing ever went wrong, and every day was a new and wonderful experience.

My favorite relative was my cousin June. She lived in the Pocono Mountains, and I only saw her once or twice a year. But we got along really well. We both liked to roller skate and would always go to the rink in Scranton, PA, whenever my parents had the money to go and visit. She was a few years older than me.

Also, Michael and Jennifer Kounnas, I wrote to them since I was fourteen years old. I didn't think I would ever meet them and then Michael came to visit from England. We had a wonderful time after writing back and forth for almost fifty years.

February 2, 2011

Back to testimonies about how great God is. We had our 2010 taxes done today with H & R Block. They wanted to charge us $305.00 to send them out. Are they crazy? We owe Federal taxes in the amount of $1158.00 and State taxes in the amount of $120.00. So, I called the IRS after praying for favor, and the man told me they could reduce this price to $230.00. Isn't God good! More like,

> *Wonderful, wonderful Jesus is to me*
> *Counselor, Prince of Peace,*
> *Mighty God is He.*
> *Saving me, keeping me from all sin and shame,*
> *Wonderful is my Redeemer, praise His name.*
>   ("Wonderful, Jesus Is to Me
>   by Haldor Lillenas, 1924" 2020)

That is a favorite song of mine. I need to go to sleep now, it's late, and I'm getting sloppy.

February 9, 2011

My mom's parents were special to me. A special memory is when I would stay many whole summers with them while school was out. They were both special people—Especially my grampy Savas. He is the one who came from the Island of Cypress. He had a very deep Greek accent. His cooking I remember the most as being the best food I ever ate anywhere. He made salads from everything in his garden, including real dandelion leaves. He had a wonderful garden. I'd eat the tomatoes right from the vine and strawberries that grew wild in his yard. Blackberries that were as big as my thumb, which he planted, and they grew up the back wall of his shed. Granny and Grampy would play 500 Rummy with me every day after lunch.

One special dish of food Grampy would make was just for me; it was a soft-boiled egg. He knew just how long to boil it, so the white was still hard and the yoke was soft. He would put it in a tiny egg cup upright and crack around the middle with a knife, then break the top open so I could dip my toast in the yolk. They didn't even have a toaster. So, he would toast my bread in the big gas oven. Then cut it into four long strips, which made dipping easier. To this day, I love eggs and always dip my toast in the yolk, but it grosses me out to have the white runny! Grampy and Granny were two of the greatest influences in my life. Grampy also taught me how to tie my shoes and swing on the swing set.

The saddest childhood memory I had was of hiding behind the front door when I was little because Granny Kounnas always had a small present for my sister Joy and never for me—Because Joy's middle name was Ruby, Granny's first name. When Granny died, she left stuff to everyone in her will except for me. My mother bad-mouthed me to the point that I was no good. Only God knows I never did any of the things she accused me of. I have forgiven both her and my mom because Jesus has forgiven me.

My mother never closed or locked our doors, even at night. One hot summer night, I was being awakened because we slept upstairs, and heat rises, so my room was especially hot. I remember we never had air conditioning, but we did have a big green fan in the window at the other end of the room. That fan provided no relief for me at all. I laid awake till after midnight and heard our back door open because it usually squeaked, then someone came in and started to walk upstairs. I was so afraid I didn't know what to do. Whoever that was turned around and left. Thank God!

Another scary time was when I almost drowned. I never learned to swim until I was twenty years old. There were three times I came really close to drowning. Once at Sun Oil Pool, once in an inner tube in a creek, my head went in first while my feet were still in the tube. Both times my mom pulled me out. The third time I was a teenager, and it was a pool party with the teens from the church. My so-called friends grabbed me and drugged me to the middle of the pool under the diving board, the deepest part. Then they all got out of the pool. I was going down for the third time when a small, thin girl named Diana Cross jumped in and pulled me out. She had gone through Red Cross training, thank God. But I was climbing up her to get out. She kept hollering at me to stop because I was pulling her under too. God finally gave me the grace to relax and let her save me. Glory to God for all the many times He saved me from me. The girls that took me to the deep end were not trying to hurt me. They thought I was kidding when I said I couldn't swim. My mom was on the phone when they pulled me out. She always had a seventh sense about us kids with almost everything that happened to us. I seemed to have it always with my own natural children. God gave us a special gift to know some things before they happen. I've learned to pray now to avoid the outcome or at least to make it better.

The happiest childhood memory was the times I spend with my closest childhood friend Andrea, across the creek in the woods, playing in our treehouse. I was a tomboy and loved the animals and the creek and woods around it. Then you could eat almost anything that grew wild—like the strawberries in the grass and the mulberries in the trees and didn't have to worry about chemicals.

God used to share a lot of things with me. Sometimes the gift He gave me would scare me. I remember, when God told me to pray for several children that might drown. Well, for three days, I prayed. I was at the bank on Saturday when the water rescue team left with their sirens blowing. I got cold chills. Somehow, I knew it was for the children I was praying for. Then Sunday, Nancy Colona came into the church with the front page of the Burlington County Times newspaper and showed me the cover story of how three young boys tried to swim across the Delaware River at the deepest point, which is under the Burlington Bristol Bridge. Two of the boys were related, which are my ex-husband's nephews, Kenny and Sherry's kids named David and Mike. I fell back against the wall. I couldn't believe it actually came true. All three started to drown because there was an undercurrent that they knew nothing about. David was climbing up Mike's legs. Finally, the smallest one, David, got out and flagged down a lady in her car who had a cell phone. She called the water rescue unit, which was the one I saw from the bank, and they rescued Mike, but the neighborhood friend drowned. They had to drag the river for his body. Nancy Colona told me if

I hadn't been obedient to the Holy Spirit, that all three boys could have died. All the glory to God for the gift He gave me and trusting me enough to pray.

Another time the Holy Spirit showed me a young woman trapped under a grating that looked like a storm drain. He didn't' tell me where she was, just to pray for her to be rescued. I did every night for days.

I was eating my lunch while watching a show called World Videos. In another country, a building had collapsed, the workers worked for days pulling people from the rubble. They decided to go home after three days, thinking no one was left, and if they were there, they were not alive. An angel came to one of the men at night while he was sleeping and woke him to tell him to go back to the building, which had collapsed and showed him where another person was. The cameras showed him pulling her out alive. She was behind a grating that looked like a storm drain. He put her on his back and took her to the hospital. I was amazed by the detail God had shown me for prayer and was so happy that she was saved.

March 24, 2011

Once again, I must go from the format of this book and its questions because God has so blessed and honored me. I almost can't take it all in when I think of all the ways He has blessed me. His Holy Spirit came upon me while I was in the shower to praise and worship Him in song, and then He told me to write it down. He also asked me to ask Sharon to put the notes above the words. Then I found myself in a recording studio, recording His song titled "Jesus". He never ceases to amaze me—what a wonderful God we serve.

The first and possibly largest blessing, of course, was when Jesus saved me, and I actually could call myself God's child. I belong to Him, and He is my Father. The second biggest blessing was my wonderful children. I can say the third blessing was my gifts that God bestowed into my life, like poetry, songwriting, tongues, prophecy, and interpretation of tongues. Healing too, when it pleases Him, and He wills it. Discerning of Spirits and even sometimes He tells me of future events and to pray for them. The fourth blessing and huge honor was to be chosen to raise Bethany and Ronald's children should God choose to take them both home at once. What a great honor that is. Bethany chose us, Ronald did not make that choice, which made the choice even more special. Praise the Lord for He is good. His mercies endure through all generations (Psalm 100:5). Isaac is like my own son, anyway. Since Billy and I had full care of him, the whole first year of his life, so Ronald and Bethany could work, I love him just like my own son. I know he feels his love from us also but doesn't actually know why.

It's getting very late, and I'm making mistakes in my writing, and my hand is hurting, so I'm going to bed. I will write soon again, God willing, and the creeks don't rise.

> *Now I lay me down to sleep.*
> *I pray the Lord my soul to keep.*
> *If I should die before I wake,*
> *I pray the Lord, my soul to take.*
> ("Nursery Rhyme, Thomas Fleet, 1737" 2020)

Rejoice, rejoice, rejoice, for when I go home, I will be rejoicing forevermore.

March 24, 2011

Still very late, but just something I thought of to write. It's stupid, but it's cute. People in the Lighthouse used to call Ronald Sr. and I, Barbie and Ken. My family used to call Frank and me, Honey and Dear, but Naomi was their favorite.

April 18, 2011

> *I love the song that goes like this,*
> *My hope is built on nothing less,*
> *than Jesus' blood and righteousness.*
> *I dare not trust the sweetest frame*
> *but wholly lean on Jesus' name.*
> *on Christ the solid rock I stand*
> *all other ground is sinking sand,*
> *all other ground is sinking sand.*
> ("My Hope Is Built on Nothing Less
> by Edward Mote, 1834" n.d.)

Since the Holy Spirit gave me the song "Jesus" to write, it's been wonderful. Saturday, Bethany and I went to the recording studio to record the demo. It was great to hear her sing my song. She has the voice of an angel. I can't wait for the final recording. I also had a very high honor or blessing when Bethany decided to make a last will and testament, in case she and Ronald ever died together. In it, she says she wants Billy and me to raise all three of her kids. What a wonderful compliment. I lift up all the glory to God for anything good she sees in me, knowing it comes from God and His Holy Spirit.

Just an unrelated thought, some people, when you witness to them, will tell you they don't believe in the Bible or a God that is invisible. Are they blind? God is not invisible. He is in the eyes, smiles, and the hugs and kisses of all my grandchildren. He is in the sunshine, the clouds, and in the thunder and rain. He is in every different snowflake and every different species of animal and fish. He is in the moon-light and the stars. I can see Him in your eyes and in every flower. Definitely in every rainbow, which are my favorite things He has created. He makes everything beautiful, no matter how hard we try to mess it up! When I am at my lowest and have nowhere to go, He carries my whole family and me. He blesses my kids and me, as well as Billy, my husband more than we can contain. His mercies are new every morning (Lamentations 3:23). He is always there when I need Him—A constant, faithful friend and Lord. He is my true Savior. There is nothing I am more thankful for than knowing Christ as my savior.

April 19, 2011

I got a brainstorm yesterday. I decided to "adopt" Deborah and Tom.

Ronald said, "Deborah and Tom, who?"

Ha-ha! They are my children anyway. I just want to make it official. After I told Deborah, she said, "I've always wanted you to do that." And I never knew she felt that way.

I love them and David like my own kids, but David doesn't bother with us, which is very sad. I'm going to make it official as soon as I get the court papers in the mail. Deborah is even sending me the $175.00 that I need to file. God works in mysterious ways, but always for the good. Thank you, Jesus! Good night.

> *Now I lay me down to sleep.*
> *I pray the Lord my soul to keep.*
> *If I should die before I wake,*
> *I pray the Lord, my soul to take.*
> ("Nursery Rhyme, Thomas Fleet, 1737" 2020)

This is a copy of my poem, which was recorded by Bethany, my daughter-in-law, on April 16, 2011, in Moorestown Studio. Written by me but inspired by the Holy Spirit on March 03, 2011, and copyrighted on March 28, 2011, on Candy's internet.

JESUS
Jesus, precious Jesus, You are my guiding light.

Jesus, precious Jesus, You hold me through the night.
Precious Holy Savior, You're there when I call.
You're always near me, Jesus, even when I fall.
You saved me, forgave me, You are my closest friend.
Jesus precious Savior, You're with me to the end.
You are my comfort, Jesus; You even save my tears.
You guide me through life's valley and love me through my fears.
There have been times I've wondered if You were really there.
You taught me Holy Savior, compassion and Your care.
My precious Holy Shepherd, please always help me see.
You hold me through life's journey; you've even carried me.

April 26, 2011

Dr. Palm ordered another mammogram for me last week. It's almost been a year since the breast cancer in July of 2010. But Praise God, all was clear and normal. God is good. I knew He healed me the first time, and the mammogram just confirmed it. "Many are the afflictions of the righteous, but the Lord delivers him out of them ALL!" (Psalm 34:19 NKJV).

April 28, 2011

I've have had a very lonely night tonight. It seems very selfish compared to the rest of the world. It seems like a single drop of water in an entire ocean. My feelings compared to the devastation of the world in chaos. Yesterday half of the Southern U.S. was wiped off the map by 160 tornadoes. Japan is still devastated by all the earthquakes and aftershocks. Tsunamis and hurricanes, tornadoes, and earthquakes continue to cover the globe. Earth pangs for the soon coming King. Global wars and starvation, unbelievable conditions that people are living in while we here in our little corner of the world seem to go untouched. Even though the gas and food prices sometimes skyrocket through the roof. Sickness and diseases are worse than ever before. Unemployment is at a new record high. Break-ins or home invasions seem to be at an epidemic level. Jesus is coming back to take us home soon. I'm afraid we haven't seen the worst of it all. So, my being lonely does not seem very important to all the world's disasters. Billy's birthday is tomorrow. He will be forty-six! No one seems to care about him or anyone else, just themselves. The Word of God says these will be the signs of the end. Also, that men will be lovers of self (2 Timothy 3:1–2). All you have to do is turn on the boob-tube to see that.

Speaking of the TV, David Trump is attacking President Obama about where he was born. Who cares, someone should... never mind, my opinion doesn't count.

People are dying and losing loved ones at an alarming rate. I probably will never finish this book unless it is by the grace of my father God. Either Jesus will come, or I will go to be with Him—either way, loneliness will be over. Pain and sorrow, worry and sickness will also be over. Thank God for Calvary.

If anyone is reading this book and has never asked Jesus to be their Savior and for Him to come into their heart, please do it today! Don't delay making this decision. It could be the single most important thing you ever do for yourself. No, not could be, it will be! Because when Jesus died on the cross at Calvary, He died for my sins and yours too. We can all go to Heaven when we die; it is His wish. There is no other way, so please, if Jesus isn't your Savior, ask Him now. He will abide in your heart, He will change your life, and you will live for eternity in Heaven. Only Jesus' blood can wash away our sins.

I am a grain of sand in a vast universe or a speck of dust that God created from the earth. Yet He cares about me and the desires of my heart.

It amazes me to think about all the planets and stars, galaxies, and beaches or oceans that God created. What if millions of people were on 100 other planets that we know nothing about? Wouldn't he care about them also? Some may not even be in our galaxy, yet God knows me and all the hairs on my head. He cares when I feel afraid or lonely, even when half of the world is broken apart. We cannot fathom the greatness of our God. There are no human words that can explain how great He is. His compassion and love for us are limitless. And yet He knows we need others to love us—someone with skin on them.

I can be with Billy all day and night and still be lonely. I know he never listens when I talk and never cares how I feel and is kind of like my dad was—there but never really there or here but never really here. I need someone to hold me, not just for sex, but love. I need someone to touch me even when they don't want sex. Someone to have a conversation with that will listen to me, really listen, and to who I will listen to them—someone who exactly knows what I need and like, and loves me enough to do it, not always, but once in a while. I don't think there will ever be anyone like that except

Jesus. Oh well, at least we have each other, and we are living in a place with no devastation "yet". My kids love me, and so do my grandkids. That alone is a wonderful blessing. Everyone is well and blessed by God, while the earth around us is crumbling.

May 21, 2011

Last night at Mike's Overcomers' group at Lighthouse Tabernacle, we talked about addiction victories. I also received the nicest compliment I've ever received from anyone. Sharlene was hugging me because I was crying, and she told me that she thought I was the godliest woman she had ever met. Wow! I never expected that. It took me a while, but after my head went down from being swollen with pride (ha-ha), I offered it up to my father God, where it belonged. Nothing good is in me except His Holy Spirit. Amen!

About a month ago, Ronnie Patton, who goes to the same church, Lighthouse Tabernacle, but in a different group, gave me another compliment. Almost as nice as Sharlene's. She said I encouraged her when she sees all I have been through, but I am still always smiling and always am "up". It's the joy of my Lord and Savior, Jesus Christ. Lots of things go wrong, including three hernia operations and one for breast cancer. But the joy of my

Lord is my strength (Psalm 28:7). Praise God that I am able, through God's strength and mercy, to obtain favor from Him and forever hold onto this joy.

It's almost midnight, and I have laryngitis and a sore throat. I have to see Dr. Deutsch, but it's Saturday. I can't even call his office until Monday, and he isn't even in his office until Wednesday. I also can't attend church tomorrow because I don't want to make everyone else sick, just in case I am contagious. I really want to go tomorrow, and I'm praying I will be well.

Billy's sister, Kay, called today. She said she is giving up and wants to go to Heaven. If that is true, it won't be long before she is gone, if God's merciful, and we know He is! She asked if we would keep in touch with Mark and take her kitty in. She has four cats. She wants us to have a black and white one. I think his name is Bootsey. I don't know how that is going to work out, considering we have to pay to keep him here, and Candy is allergic. I'd rather see my daughter than have anyone's cat. It's a shame to feel that way, but it's true.

I need to go to bed and get some sleep. I pray God keeps me through the night, but if He doesn't, I'll see you at the Pearly Gates someday soon. I love all of you guys more than you will ever know. I know you might miss me but never be sad because I will be with our Lord and Savior Jesus—finally home.

If there is anything, I am constantly learning in my walk with Jesus is that I am totally powerless over my life and its situations. Christ has ultimate rule and control. I can grind my teeth and worry until I'm sick and even eat myself into oblivion, and still, there is nothing I can do without God and His will for my life. I cry out to Him every day and might for Isaac, Caitlyn, Ronald, Candy, James, and everyone else.

I'm sure God hears my prayers and answers them because I belong to Him, and so do all my children and grandkids. We are His. They are only lent to their parents or me for a short while. God is good all the time. He is teaching me that I need just to leave it with Him. No matter how hard I try, He is in control, not me, and I am or was a control freak. The main reason I hate flying is that I can't fly the plane myself. At least I know some of my faults. At sixty-four years old, I should be aware of at least a few. Some others I am working on with God's help are losing weight, listening carefully to my kids, and not gossiping. That one seems to be the hardest. Even though I stop, I don't know how to 'not listen' to others gossiping. Especially Candy and Ginny. I want to tell them, but I'm afraid they will hang up the phone and not talk to me. Also, forgiveness and judging others are hard. That is a real toughie. But God knows my heart. I'm really serious about obeying Him. His word says obedience is better than sacrifice (1 Samuel 15:22).

By the way, God blessed Ronald and Bethany again in a really wonderful way. He told them to give their last $100.00 to their pastor, so they did. The same night Linda, Bethany's mom, called and said they were bringing over $100.00 from them, but when they arrived, she gave them $220.00 instead. God always outdoes everything you can give. Always!

My prayers now are for James, who just told me he has cirrhosis of the liver or "black lung". I know God can heal him, and at the same time, He can work in James's heart to draw him closer. He worked for the fiberglass company, and Ronald said he was the only one that didn't wear a face mask. God, please help him, He is my son, but he belongs to You!

Nighty, night—I love you guys!

June 13, 2011

Praise the Lord! For He is good, and His mercies endure through all generations (Psalms 100:5). The Holy Spirit placed on my heart today, actually it was yesterday, to call that man, Danny. He owns the beautiful blue and white Jesus painting I want for my CD cover. After he emailed Bethany and told her we could purchase it for $800.00, God told me to ask him to use it and pay him 10% of our gross sales. So, I found him in Florida and spoke to him personally. He agreed to send me a paper to sign, then send it back to him, and he would release the original called, *I Asked Jesus* to Disc Makers to put on my CD. Praise the Lord! Nothing else would do. It had to be Jesus and the three crosses with a light in the clouds shinning on Him. It will prolong the final copy, but it will be worth it.

June 14, 2011

Here is a poem I wrote inspired by the Holy Spirit on June 7, 2011.

God's Gift – A Writer

I take a pen and paper, and I go inside my nook.
I emerge just like a butterfly,
But then I have a book.
I write because inside of me,
God created a special part.
Of all the blessings He gave to me,
This one turned out to be my heart.
Rivers of joy in abundance,
Flow from every part of me.

Because of Jesus and His Word,
He finally made me see;
I can do nothing, without Him,
All my tries become insane.
To worry or to work to help,
Is stupid and in vain.
His Word works, if you work it,
And believe within your heart,
There was a reason He created you,
And in God's plan, you have a part.
God's miracle, one body,
Each one a separate skill.
Someday will be perfected,
That day comes within His Will.
We will operate as one, as He created us to be.
His precious Bride come forth,
And the Bride Groom we will finally see.
The butterfly emerges from that dank, dark cocoon.
There is nothing that can stop us,
And it's coming very soon.
(Naomi Jean Ortiz 2011)

July 1, 2011

The man who painted my CD picture, *I Asked Jesus*, is in the hospital in Florida. His name is Danny. His wife called me, she was so kind, she asked me which one I needed for the CD cover, and I told her, *I Asked Jesus*. She sent it in an email that night to the CD Makers, and no money had exchanged hands yet. I couldn't believe how good God is. I did ask when I prayed, and I bound all hindering spirits because it seemed like it was taking forever to be made. I figured the enemy of our souls did not want the song to come out. Oh, praise the name of Jesus! We all know who won that conflict. All I've had to do was read the end of the Bible, thank you, Lord, for winning the victory for us at Calvary. I am praying for Danny, and I hope he is doing better.

There are so many new testimonies of how good God is; I don't know where to start! First, I felt another lump on my right breast. My doctor sent me for an ultrasound because I just had a mammogram in June, and it was normal. Praise God! So, the hospital did an ultrasound two days ago, and the nurse had to call the radiologist into my room because she couldn't find anything. Well, neither could he, praise the Lord for He is good, all the time! His mercies endure through all generations (Psalm 100:5). Amen.

Baby Emily, Joy's grandbaby, not only survived her heart operation, but she came home the next day and is doing very well. She was born a twin with a hole in her heart.

Ronald and Bethany did their own taxes for 2010 and had H&R Block check their work. They got another $2,000.00. Praise God! The Lord told Ronald, after paying off their bills, to give their last $100 to their preacher, which I explained earlier. *What a Wonderful Savior:* What a wonderful Savior is Jesus, my Jesus. What a wonderful Savior is Jesus, my Lord. Amen, how majestic is thy name, oh Lord.

August 1, 2011

I don't feel much like writing tonight. It's very late, and I feel very sad. I don't even know why I feel this way. I feel like no one loves me except, of course, Jesus. I'm sure He loves me. I guess that should be enough, but sometimes I need a hug. Stupid me, thinking that having a husband would ensure me of getting hugged when that was the dumbest thing I ever decided. Billy won't even move an inch for me ever—Never, never, never. It's always tomorrow or when he's ready, which is usually never. James makes it worse by getting mad at me for petty things, I say. You love your kids all your life, and you're lucky if one or two, like me out of seven kids, love you back and really show it. Candy tries, but her own family is overwhelming. I can usually always count on her, Deborah, or Ronald; at least I have three out of seven. Some people have no one. And Ginny, my best friend and prayer partner, is so old and so worried about her dog that she has no time for me either. It all boils down to the same thing. The only one you can ever count on is Jesus.

On a lighter note, I have been getting blessed by God a lot lately. I have no right to have a pity party, but somethings still hurt.

I just gave my life testimony Friday night at the Overcomers' meeting at Light House Tabernacle. They changed their name to Addictions Victorious. It was definitely God's will to have it that night as opposed to June. I was first upset that Mike changed the night from June to July, but Mike didn't... God did. Never be upset over delays. 99% of them are divine delays of God. In June there were eleven or twelve people there. In July, there were forty, and after it was over, several people were touched by my testimony. One new lady, Pat and Bruce Gifford's daughter, came up to me and hugged me and started to cry. She said I never knew anyone else could be like me. She touched my heart, and so did Andrea's compliment. Andrea said she wished she had heard me speak a year ago. All glory to God for He is good, and His mercy endures forever, and His timing is perfect (Psalm 100:5). Also, the steps of a good man or woman are ordered by the Lord (Psalm 37:23). The whole night was a blessing. Pastor McKenna was also there too.

Billy's sister, Kay, had her Neurosurgery on her brain tumor, and it was successful. I was so shocked when Rosie called and said she is awake and talking. Praise God!

The miracles never end. John Alden, Holly's boyfriend, gave us $1,000 to pay off our taxes so that we would have no more penalties or interest. We are paying him back in $300 payments, which he already has one for August, one for September, and another for October. Then the last $100 in November. Glory to God.

Also, Ursula, in Dr. Holiday's office, took off our $70 for us from my breast cancer operation. I know that was God! Good night.

Our Church Reunion

Mom Song:

It took a miracle to hang the stars in place.
It took a miracle to place the world in space.
But when he saved my sound cleansed and made
  me whole,
It took a miracle of love and grace.
  ("It Took a Miracle" n.d.)

> Bible Covenant Baptist Church Fellowship
> Gathering. June 22, 2011
> Shady Maple in Lancaster, PA

August 3, 2011

> Song:

> *To God be the glory, great things He has done.*
> *So, loved He the world, that He gave us His Son.*
> *Who yielded His life, an atonement for sin,*
> *And opened the life gates that all my go in.*
> *Praise the Lord. Praise the Lord. Let the earth hear His voice.*
> *Praise the Lord. Praise the Lord. Let the people rejoice.*
> *Oh, come to the Father through Jesus His Son,*
> *and give Him the glory, great things He has done.*
>> ("To God Be the Glory
>> by Fanny Crosby, 1875" n.d.)

August 31, 2011

> Here is something else I wrote:

> *Wonderful Marvelous Jesus,*
> *You are the King of my soul*

> You made me and watched every step I took,
> While you were making me whole.
>
> He is a shield to those who walk uprightly. He guards the path of justice and preserves the way of His saints. Then you will understand righteousness and justice, equity and every good path.
>
> (Proverbs 2:7–9 NKJV)

Special note: Last Tuesday at Beacons, I was asked to lead the singing. It was Margie's month, but she was ill. However, four or five days before I was asked. The Holy Spirit told me to pick out four songs to lead. I was tickled pink to know that God still speaks to me! Praise His name.

August 31, 2011

We just arrived home on Monday from our four-day trip to Ohio with Ronald and Bethany, Isaac, and the twins. God really blessed our socks off on this trip. Friday night, when we left, we had to stop to sleep at 1:00 a.m. We almost found no rooms anywhere because of Hurricane Irene that was supposed to hit N.J. Saturday late into Sunday a.m. So, everyone had the same idea we did, to travel inland. Ronald and Bethany's trip had been planned two months before this. We finally got a room, complete with yellow sheets and dead bugs, but by then, it was 3:00 a.m., so we had to sleep. The next morning, we had breakfast and set out again for Ohio. Bethany's aunt called Ronald on his cell phone in the car. She asked where we were and what time we would be there. Ronald told her about all the delays we had, and when we would be there. She responded, "Forget it. Turn around and go home. We expected you at 1:00 p.m." We wouldn't be there till around 4:00 p.m. or 5:00 p.m. So, we got off at the next exit to talk about what we should do. Bethany was crying, and Ronald was mad. Then the crazy witch's husband, Victor, called. Ronald said to go to Western Union; he was wiring us $500. Praise the Lord for He is good all the time. The second blessing was that we just happened to get off at the Bedford, PA exit where Candy and Danny had a reservation in a Quality Inn and couldn't use it because Caitlyn wouldn't go—Right where we had parked to talk. The third blessing is we looked across the street, and there was the Quality Inn where they had their reservations set, which was now ours. Sometimes I can't believe how good God is. Especially with the little things. So, our trip was unusually good, spite the fact that Bethany's aunt told us off. God is good all the time, especially when you need Him most. Jesus never fails.

September 10, 2011, Saturday

Billy is working over-time, praise God! Another answer to our prayers. His sister Kay called me early today, and we talked about how good Jesus is for about half an hour. Then she told me how she fell into a deep sleep inside that awful round MRI machine. While she was sleeping, Jesus came to her, and it was so peaceful and wonderful that she didn't want to wake up. She told me she was ready to go home. She also gave me a wonderful compliment, which I lift up to God. She told me that I was like a "spiritual Candy dish," that someone like her could pull a piece of Candy out of it to be ministered to. All glory to God, for there is nothing good within me except His Holy Spirit.

I just remembered to write about *Moments with Mary*. That is a monthly newsletter that Mary, my old Sunday school teacher, writes, prints, and sends to hundreds of people.

October 19, 2011

I still have a lot to learn about Christ and His compassion for others and His tender mercies. Four days ago, on Saturday, I was getting out of Candy's van when

I was verbally attacked by this woman who lived behind me in the courtyards. I didn't even know her name, and apparently, unknown to me, has lived here for nine years, where she parked in the spot where Mike, our maintenance man, had installed my handicap post. So, she went ballistic. She was like a crazy person who escaped from the nuthouse! She acted like I put the post in and that I knew she had parked there, which I didn't. I was so shocked at all the harsh words, and I didn't' even know how to respond. She was even digging the post out of the ground like it was her own property! Well, God's Word says to pray for your enemies, so I did. I prayed for her salvation. She is definitely lost. I also made a report to the police. The children were playing at the playground while she was screaming at me, and they came to me when it was over. They said, "She is a mean lady; she hollers at us too." It's a shame they had to see an adult acting like a crazy person.

November 2, 2011

God's Word, the Bible, says life is a vapor (James 4:14) like your breath on a cold day or the steam from a pot of hot water. Here for a few brief seconds, then gone. "Boy, that is self-evident to me." It seems like just yesterday I was playing hide and seek in my mom and dad's front yard. It was dusk and Andrea and Susan were there with my sister, brothers, and me. I cried till I had no more tears left when my little white fluffy puppy, snowball, got hit by a car. I played Monopoly every day for over a week after school with my friend. It never ended. I traded feathers with a boy from my class named David Wilson. I climbed trees and made tree houses with Andrea. I ate a whole quart jar of mayonnaise with Andrea and two knives. I held my first son James in my arms for the first time and was amazed at how wonderfully beautiful he was. I had never seen anything more beautiful.

Then I turn around, and now I am old, and it was only like yesterday I was catching lightning bugs in a jar. All of God's Word is true, especially when it refers to life as being a breath (James 4:14). Soon I will not be here any longer, but with my savior and Lord Jesus for all eternity.

Sometimes I can't wait to go home, and other times I love being here with my grandchildren and, believe it or not, even Billy. I do feel like I'm a sojourner, just traveling through this hurried life, on my way to the next life. Sometimes all the mundane things I do here seem such a waste of time when all that matters is what I do for others and Christ.

Only one life will soon be past. Only what's done for Christ will last.

("Quote by C.T. Studd" n.d.)

So then why bother? I guess because this is life and it's a gift from God, what we do with it matters to Him.

Heaven and earth may pass away, but Jesus never fails (Matthew 24:35).

November 19, 2011

Defender, My Healer, You are my King. Praise the Lord!

Yesterday was Candy's birthday. We all went to Red Lobster, even though we can't afford much on that menu. God made a way. Even though Danny is out of work, God made a way. Also, yesterday the Courtyards office called me to let me know that Billy and I qualify for Moderate Income Housing, Christa was the girl that called. I went to the library to apply over the internet, and a lady there helped me print out the application to sign and send. Praise God! If we are accepted, our rent will go from $1025 to $860. Isn't He wonderful! That is an answer to prayer.

Holly called me last week and told me a story I could barely believe. Isaac, her youngest son, is three. She accidentally fell asleep on the couch, and he took her plastic flowers and went into the kitchen and turned on the stove and lit the flowers on fire. He carried them into the living room while they were burning and said, "Mommy." Holly woke up, thank God, and saw the flowers in his hands-on fire and grabbed them, ran into the kitchen, and put them in the sink to put them out. She got some small burns from the melting plastic, and her rugs were ruined, but the fire never touched Isaac. Praise the Lord. I know God protected him. He could have caught on fire, and she could have slept through it. Glory to God... for His love for all of us, especially our children. Truly His mercies are new every morning Lamentations 3:23).

November 23, 2011

Another blessing! Praise the Lord. Isaac Sr. found out we couldn't come to the DOMA (my husband's employer) Christmas party in Virginia Beach because we didn't have the money for the room. So, he called the Marriott on the water and paid for our room, and even paid for our breakfast the next day. Isn't God wonderful? Yes. More than we can contain or think—all the time. I can't wait to go to the party and see Isaac again.

Tomorrow is Thanksgiving. Boy, do we have a lot to thank God for. More than anyone I know. A song came to my heart this morning while I was praying called *Change My Heart*. It goes;

> *Change my heart, oh God.*
> *Make it ever true.*
> *Change my heart, oh God.*
> *May I be like You.*
> *You are the potter. I am the clay.*
> *Mold me and make me.*
> *This is what I pray.*
> *Change my heart, oh God.*
> *Make it ever true.*
> *Change my heart, oh God.*
> *May I be like you.*
> *May I be like you.*
>
> ("Change My Heart Oh Lord by Eddie Espinos, 1982" n.d.)

Thank you seems like such a small word for all He has done. So, listen to my heart, oh, Lord.

Song:

> *Thank you, Lord, for saving my soul*

Thank you, Lord, for making me whole.
Thank you, Lord, for giving to me,
Thy great salvation, so rich and free...
                ("Thank You, Lord
                by Seth and Bessie Sykes" n.d.)

Last night was the Overcomers' meeting at Light House Tabernacle. Many, many people old and young, needed help and lots of prayer. I am truly blessed compared to what they have gone through or are going through now. I especially need to pray for a young boy named Brad, and I don't remember her name, but she sat next to Norma and me. Jesus, Lord and Savior, please help these people. They need your strength and your deliverance in their lives. Nefertiti is Linda's daughter, and Bethany needs their kid's home. Please give them favor for the sake of their children. Help us all. We need you, Lord. Father God, in Jesus' name, please hear our prayers. We can't make it without You. Candy needs your help too, and so do I. We need You to cover our children, and my grandbabies, to hedge us in all around, cancel the schemes and plots of the enemy over our lives and shelter us in Your rock. Cover us with the blood of Jesus, our Savior, and continue to be merciful to us, Your children. We are surely sinners, saved by Your marvelous grace.

December 14, 2011

    To God, be the glory for things He has done. It's eleven days till Jesus' Birthday! People are so angry and mean. I was at Walmart yesterday, and there was a young boy, maybe eighteen or nineteen, ringing the bell for the Salvation Army. He looked frozen to the ground. As I passed, I said to him, "You look frozen."
    "Only my feet," he said.
    God put on my heart to buy him a hot chocolate at Subway. I went in, and they only had cold chocolate. I asked the clerk to heat it in the microwave. He did, and it got nice and hot. I also got him a small pizza and a gift card. I wrote on it, "To an angel, from a friend." He was so happy to get the chocolate, and he kept thanking me. Oh, I also wrote, "Jesus loves you" on the card envelope. I wanted God to get all the credit for the idea.

December 25, 2011, Christmas Day—6:30 a.m.
    Happy Birthday, Jesus! Wonderful Lord and Savior, closest friend, and confidant. Lover of my soul. Praise Your Holy Name. Luke 2:14 (KJV), "Glory to God in the highest, and on earth peace, goodwill toward men."
    Christmas Blessings or gifts that God gave me today. How about our God, He gives us gifts on His birthday. We should emulate Him.

1. A preacher Tom knew, gave him $1000 to come to NJ.
2. Isaac Sr. paid for our Virginia room and breakfast, and on the way home on the bus, God broke the sound on the DVD player. In answer to my prayer and a safe trip. The bus line was called "Majesty".
3. The day before payday Aunt Milla sent us a Christmas card and $20 that we really needed, and I found $5 on the floor of the store, Dollar Tree.
4. Ronald and Bethany needed two new tires desperately, and my friend Ginny bought and had them installed for them.
5. I waited five months for a state check to come in for babysitting Ronald's kids while he and Bethany took Foster Care classes. Jesus knew when I needed it most and brought the check in just when my tooth broke. I owed Dr. Budd $100, and he charged me $98, and the check was for $200.
6. Billy got a $400 bonus at work, after taxes, it was $250.
7. All my children and grandbabies are healthy and well. Praise the Lord!
8. Billy, I, and our moms are healthy and well.

9. God supplies ALL our needs, according to His riches in Glory.
10. Greater is He that is in us, than he that is in the world (1 John 4:4).
11. "I can do ALL things through Christ who strengthens me" (Philippians 4:13 NKJV).

December 26, 2011

> *Often in the stillness,*
> *I pause to hear His voice*
> *And in sharing that sweet moment,*
> *I find reasons to rejoice.*
> *Praise God!*

December 29, 2011

Almost the end of this year has passed. A new one beginning again. I found this poem called 'Broken Chain' in a magazine and need to write it for Todd and my Dad and all those who have gone before me.
Broken Chain

> *We never knew that morning*
> *That God was going to call your name.*
> *In life, we loved you dearly*

In death, we do the same.
It broke our hearts to lose you,
You did not go alone.
For part of us went with you
The day God called you home.
You left us peaceful memories
Your love is still our guide.
And though we cannot see you
You are always at our side.
Our family chain is broken
And nothing seems the same.
But as God calls us one by one,
The chain will link again.

(Tranmer n.d.)

December 29, 2011

God has never left me. He is still by my side. Today I was very sad because of Christmas, and my family decided not to see me and lots of other things I expected from people that I love and just are never there for me. I need to realize that only Jesus can meet my needs. No one will ever love me or care for me as He does, so it is silly to expect anyone to.

Here is a wonderful page from my *Daily Bread Devotional*, which speaks about rejoicing in our Lord. No matter what life has dished out for us. No matter darkness, rain, hatred, or even cancer. God is sovereign, and He knows exactly what He is doing at all times. We need to "rejoice in the Lord always: and again, I say rejoice" (Philippians 4:4 KJV). We have to make a choice to rejoice.

December 31, 2011, New Year's Eve

God is good—all the time. Once again, He answered my prayers for Caitlyn. She is only fourteen, and Danny said she could accompany Miguel, her friend and his parents to New York City for the ball drop in Times Square. I know that was bad news, and she could get taken by someone or, at the very minimum, lost. So, I prayed God would stop the trip, and He did. For whatever reason, it was canceled by Miguel's parents. He was very upset, but I was praising and thanking God. I love Caitlyn and pray for her every day. God knows best. He knew before I prayed or even before time began that it was not a good idea to go. His will is always done.

> *You have set the boundaries of the earth and you have made summer and winter.*
> (Psalms 74:17 NLT)

CHAPTER 3

January 26, 2012

When it seems like all is lost, in my darkest hour, Jesus shines His light on all that is evil. First, it's just a glimmer, and then it is a rainbow. Since Christmas, I have felt defeated and depressed. Then I started to remember the faithfulness and goodness of my God. Every time the enemy came in like a flood, God set up a standard against him. In His time, not mine.

Jesus also said, "...The little foxes that spoil the vines..." (Song of Solomon 2:15 NKJV). What this means to me is that the little things in life might not matter if there was one alone, like losing Billy's van registration, but seven, eight, or nine problems piled on top of one another is not fun. The enemy also knows that, although sometimes he has nothing to do with anything, it's just called life.

Here is the list of what made me sad:
1. James is not speaking to me since before and including Christmas.
2. Caitlyn is having headaches and a tumor in her brain.
3. The respiratory infection that I had and was on steroids, and I ache all over.
4. I have constant pain in my right side, and it hurts to drive.
5. We lost the registration for the van, which we eventually found.
6. Billy's diabetes is getting worse, and he is not taking care of himself.
7. Our insurance will not cover Billy for a preexisting condition.
8. Isaac being on Pulmicort steroids every day, twice a day, just to stay out of the hospital.
9. I am not able to go to Friday p.m. Overcomers' because of Norma.
10. Ronald and Bethany's new car is not working. They had to call the lemon-lawyer.
11. We applied for Moderate Income Housing and were told we qualified, and then we were denied.

There was more I took them out because enough is enough. I will write again with answers to all our prayers because God answers prayers, always.

February 13, 2012

The day before Valentine's Day. Jesus is my valentine. First love, always loves and loves last.

Almost all of the eleven things that were going wrong, on the previous page, have been righted or made better by God. He always turns all thing things the enemy means for evil into good. He always sets up a standard when the enemy comes in like a flood. This is good, but some may not understand the jargon, so maybe explain this a little further would be good.

Two of my important prayers were just answered. My son James talked to me almost for an hour on Friday. It warmed my heart to hear him tell me about his problems. I only hope and pray these things will draw him to Christ and that God will heal his lungs and sinus out of His abounding mercy.

Also, Ronald and Bethany's twins, Savannah and Alexis, were dedicated yesterday at the New Hope Bible Church in Riverside. A long-time prayer of mine answered in that occurrence. They are three and a half years old now and also need healing of sinus, ears, and upper respiratory infection. Christ died to set the captives free and provide healing and deliverance for everyone. Jesus is my Healer, and also Isaac's and the twins, as well as Caitlyn's. Jesus never fails! "Heaven and earth may pass away," but Jesus never fails! (Matthew 24:25 NIV).

March 1, 2012

Dear Lord and Savior, it's been a while since I wrote to You, but it hasn't changed my love. You draw me closer every day to the heart of God. The studying we are doing in *Becoming a Woman of Influence* is amazing. It's like a steppingstone to the desire in my heart to speak to younger women about Your will for their lives, which has been my desire now for many years. If You tarry in coming to take us home, I'd like to speak about my life and Your love.

Thank you for that beautiful card that You placed on Bethany's heart to send me. It means the world to me to be appreciated. Thank you that Ronald and Bethany are teaching the youth. Please send healing to them and their household and teach them how to stay covered.

Thank you, Lord, for Linda L, and putting her on my heart to send a card to and the "hope" bookmarker. When she called to tell me how much it meant to her, it warmed my heart.

Thank you, Lord, for turning my son James's heart around to speak to me again. I need him in my life—such wonderful answers to prayers. Thank you for restoring Tom and Sherry's marriage and family, and for the new home you gave them from David in Little River, South Carolina. Please help them to make the money they need to keep their home.

Thank you for Caitlyn's last doctor visit, and that she is doing better. Please help her to go to school with a desire in her heart and to be well enough to finish and graduate. Bless her medication and Isaac's to their bodies Lord, with no lasting side effects. Thank you for the little bird that is singing outside my window.

> *When I am on my knees in prayer,*
> *I know I'll find you there.*
> *Your promises are true, and mercy is always new.*
> *No one ever loved me so, and I'm sure you know.*
> *My heart is true; I too love You and will never let*
> *you go.*

Special thanks to You for all the help You have been sending us through Danny. He fixed a slow leak in my Volkswagen bug by putting a new stem in the tire. He bought me a cell-phone case for the new phone Deborah got for me. Praise the Lord. He paid for my wooden roses and my black fur coat from the thrift store, as well as my salad at the Red Lobster. He planted a holly tree for me and picked up the heart-shaped bamboo plant that I wanted for Valentine's Day. He hired Billy to work with him on a home move and only worked him for five hours and gave him $100 that we really needed for food.

Ronald used his food stamps to buy us pork chops and potatoes and sausage and lots of other food. Praise the Lord!

Our clock in the hallway is playing *Oh Little Town of Bethlehem*. It's almost Easter—Resurrection Day. But the songs still sound beautiful. I'm so glad Billy put the batteries in the Christmas clock.

I almost forgot to thank you for meeting "Chrystal" at the thrift store in Burlington and bringing her and Sue to our Addictions Victorious Meeting on Friday night. Thank you for crossing my life's path with people who need you. Thank you for opening my mouth to witness to them, and thank you for my new friend Cynthia, who really loves our church and our Fellowship. She is a good friend. I needed her as much as she needed me.

It has been really nice getting to know my sister Joy also. A long time coming, but never too late. Thank you, Lord Jesus. I appreciate you and all you've done.

March 5, 2012—3:05 a.m.

Praise God, from whom all blessings flow. Praise Him all creatures here below. Praise Him all above ye Heavenly hosts. Praise Father, Son, and Holy Ghost. Amen.

("Hymn: Praise God, from Whom All Blessings Flow by Thomas Ken, 1673" 2020)

Again, and again God answers my humble, tiny, unimportant, except to me prayers. Unfathomable how the One true God, mighty is He, who created the universe with His spoken Word, would even care about me, one grain of sand, and my prayers. The human brain cannot even begin to grasp the awesomeness of our God. Just think of all the grains of sand on all the beaches in the universe or even "one," how numerous and uncountable, except for God. Yet, I am like that grain of sand, and He considers me... amazing! He loves me. He is merciful to me, He communicates with me if I bother to listen. He even cares about the desires of my heart. My mind cannot grasp His awesome greatness. To be human in the presence of our mighty God is like one of us dying for an ant or a worm. But what He did doesn't even compare.

Thank you, my Lord and my God, for taking my place and shedding your holy blood for me, so that I could be free and saved from an eternal hell. Thank you for answering prayers. Candy, Danny, and Caitlyn came to worship service today, and I wanted to cry. I was so happy. I love you, Lord, because you show me every day how much you love me. There is nothing sweeter than to know You and walk with You and talk with You. Sweeter as the days go by! I can't even put into words how wonderful and thankful I am to know You as my Lord and Savior. I can't wait till I meet you face to face and sit at your feet to be with you for eternity.

March 11, 2012, Sunday—6:00 a.m.

Hosanna, Hosanna in the Highest. Hosanna, Hosanna, Hosanna in the Highest. I woke up with praise on my heart. Precious Savior and Lord, thank you for involving me, in these end days, about witnessing to your lost souls. Nothing I love better to do than to help the Master of my soul "round up" all those who need salvation. You caused our paths to cross and opened my heart and mouth to witness to them. Cynthia is coming to our church, at Beacon's every week and loves praise and worship. Then Crystal, who you caused me to meet in the "thrift store" down Burlington by Cafe Gallery. Crystal is going every week now to Mike's group, Friday p.m., for the Celebrate Recovery class. Wonderful people in our group who were once addicted to drugs, alcohol, or something, and God has cleaned them up. Praise His name. Now, Sue, who was our waitress for years at Golden Dawn, is also coming. You put Ronald Sr.'s old friend on my heart of who to pray for, for salvation, and to come to Friday nights. I hope someday he comes. I mainly hope that he is saved.

The sun is rising now. I'm praying all my children and grandchildren will be in church today. Please hear my prayer, oh, Mighty God, in Jesus' name. I want to include my stepchildren, too, in this prayer. My prayer is also to open the eyes and heart and mind of my husband, Billy. That someday before You come to take us home, he will totally drop all this pride and stubbornness and worship and pray with me. Only God can make a tree, and only God can change a heart like He changed mine.

On a lighter note, I wanted to remember all the laughter and fun times we've had, especially with Isaac. He said that he "saw God die," and I said, "Where?"

And he said, "On Netflix."

And last night, he needed underwear and the clean clothes were in Ronald and Bethany's room, and it was locked. He asked me to go in and get some, and I couldn't reach the key on top of the door ledge. So, he went into the bathroom and got out the step stool so I could stand on it and reach the key. He is so funny. I can't help having two favorite grandbabies. Now I know why my mom preferred William because he grew up in her house. And Isaac grew up in ours, especially the whole first year of his life, while Ronald and Bethany worked. Billy and I had him every day for over a year.

As for Caitlyn, she grew up in my home on Northampton Drive, so I'm closer to her and Isaac than any of my other grandchildren. I can't help it. That is just how it goes. I love the twins and Johnathan and James Jr. as well as all my twenty grandbabies, but I'll always go out of my way for Caitlyn and Isaac. They have a special place in my heart.

Yesterday a squirrel ate through our kitchen screen and ate my fresh made wheat rolls that I bought at the Amish store for dinner. He heard me coming from the bedroom and quickly retreated back out the hole in the screen. He spared our dinner and left little black footprints on my toaster cover. Ha-ha!

My hand is tired of writing. I've been praying for extra money to pay off our credit cards and bills. Sue shared on Friday night about an antique place that has rooms and cabinets for rent in Burlington. I am going tomorrow to see if I can rent one cheap and sell all my junk. God always makes a way of escape, even if you did it to yourself. He is so wonderful and good to my kids and me. We've never gone hungry and always, always had blessings upon blessings poured out to us. First, last night God dropped a free ticket off to Ronald and

Bethany for the flower show. Just before they left to go and Sherry came back to Tom, and they got a beautiful home in Little River, South Carolina. Their home is right by David and Myrtle Beach, and God even got Tom a new job. Isn't He wonderful? Blessings so wonderful and numerous, I almost forgot some of them because we tend to focus on the hard parts of life. I want to see the cup half full, not half empty. If my God fills it, it's not half full, it's running over because He loves us so much. I love you too, Lord. Bless Your holy name.

April 6, 2012, Good Friday

My precious Savior hung on the cross for me today. He took all my sin, sickness, diseases, pain, and sorrow on His body on the tree of Calvary. There is nothing I can do to repay Him except to try and live every day as Christ-like as possible and give Him my whole life. There was no greater love than our Father God's, and there will never be. He loves me, unconditionally. He forgives me. He knows just what I like and always gives me the desires of my heart. He forgives me when I ask. He is patient and kind and loves like no other lover. He is my best friend. And when I am too weak to go on, He carries me. Praise His name, for He is more than worthy to be praised.

Our long-time prayer was finally answered for my mom. Monday 4-21-12, four days ago, we finally got mom in Fair Acres. She didn't want to go and called everyone she knew to help her, but everyone knows she needed full-time care. For the first time in years, she is clean, and her bed is clean, she has three good, nutritious meals a day. God is always good. We just have to wait for His timing. For everything, there is a season and a time under heaven (Ecclesiastes 3:1).

April 19, 2012

Mom had a stroke yesterday afternoon. She couldn't talk when Bart called her. Fair Acres, where she lives now, took her to the ER at Riddle Memorial. By the time Joy and Bart got there, she was already improving, and when I called, she could talk again. Mom is eighty-eight today and will be eighty-nine years old in September. They said she couldn't swallow, but I'm not sure they know. Today is Thursday, and they were going to keep her overnight just to watch her. I want to go to see her today, but I can't drive both ways. So, I have to find a driver or wait till Billy gets home from work at 4:00 p.m. Just don't want her to lie around and suffer. If God has plans to take her, may it be swiftly, like he did my dad.

P.S. Lexie had her tummy X-rayed for a penny she swallowed. She stopped pooping two days later, but God answered our prayers once again. She seems to be ok now. She may have to be X-rayed again to see if it passed.

Also, the day before she swallowed the penny, both the twins ate a whole box of Pepcid AC. Ronald took them to the ER, and they gave one twin liquid charcoal. They are both fine. Praise the Lord. Remember His words that say,

> ...these signs shall follow them that believe; In my name they shall cast out devils; they shall speak in new tongues; if they drink (or eat) any deadly thing, it shall not hurt them; They shall lay hands on the sick, and they shall recover.
>
> (Mark 16:17–18 KJV)

> *And we know that all things work together for good to them that love God, to them who are the called according to his purpose.*
>
> (Romans 8:28 KJV)

April 28, 2012, Saturday

Mom is back to Fair Acres, and totally well, praise be to God. Ecclesiastes 3:1 says, "to every thing there is a season and a time to every purpose under Heaven" (KJV).

God's word is always true because if Mom was not in Fair Acres when she had her stroke, she would be lying on the floor of her house, possibly for two or three days alone. So, the Lord got her in there just in time. He is always on time, never late.

Candy and Dan and James, my oldest son, went to see her and me this past Thursday. It was so nice to see family and my mom. She had a stomachache. I think that she is getting far too many pills for things she doesn't even need—especially potassium, which is deadly in large amounts. Monday I am going to talk to the doctor—Doctor Anna Maria Jamal.

Last night, April 27th, everyone came over to visit. Ronald and Bethany, Isaac, the twins, and the new foster child Jayden. Candy and Caitlyn. Isaac drew me two beautiful pictures, and Savannah said: "Nanny, I love you."

That meant the world to me. Ronald brought me a beautiful tiny shadow box to hang on the wall. It was almost like Christmas. God provided food to feed everyone also. The day was so beautiful; I almost thought it was my last day, and I wouldn't have cared if it was. I was so happy. Thank you, Lord, for the valleys, but thank you so very much for the mountain tops.

April 29, 2012, Sunday, Billy's Forty-Seventh Birthday

We had a wonderful day today celebrating Billy's birthday until we came home and found a message on our phone that Mom had another stroke and was rushed to Riddle Memorial Hospital. Bart told Lorraine to tell me she didn't look like she was going to make it. But the doctors hadn't even seen her yet. Well, she revived again and was well enough to holler at Holly for taking all her jewelry and my train. I don't care anymore about all the stuff Holly stole from Mom—That is between her and God. I do wish someone would tell John he is in danger that Holly only wants his money. But I can't do it, the only thing I can do is pray that the things that are hidden will be exposed to the light and that John's eyes will be opened before it is too late.

Today I learned that Granny Kounnas, my mom's mom, had twenty-one or twenty-two strokes before she passed. Mom has only had four so far. I just keep praying that God takes her without any suffering. Mom is a tough old bird. She will probably be here for a while if they adjust her medications properly.

> *Good night, sweet dreams.*
> *I love you, Father God.*
> *I love you, Holy Spirit.*
> *I love you, Jesus.*
> *Keep me safe and close to your heart.*
> *If I should die before I wake, I pray, sweet Lord, my soul you'll take.*
> ("Nursery Rhyme, Thomas Fleet, 1737" 2020)

May 6, 2012, Sunday—6:20 a.m.

Mom went home to be with Jesus. Praise the Lord, for He is good, His mercies endure through all generations (Psalm 100:5). What else can you say except that Mom had a long and full healthy life. She would have been eighty-nine in September. God blessed her all the way to the end. We all prayed that He wouldn't allow her to lay around and suffer, and He didn't. Just like my dad, she was taken quickly. God answered our prayers once again and was full of compassion and mercy.

My kids have been good to me. Ronald took us to lunch right after church to the Golden Corral. It was great to be with the kids, Ronald, Candy, Isaac, the twins, Caitlyn, the new little guy Jayden, and Jr. I'm so thankful to God that I have wonderful children, stepchildren, and grandchildren. God has truly blessed me, abundantly, all my life.

Tomorrow, May 7th, Joy and Bart have to pick out a casket and try to leave enough money to feed everyone who comes to the church. I pray God will lead and guide them by His Holy Spirit to do well and that all will go as best as it can. I know it will because God is good all the time. He never fails me or us. God is love, and love never fails.

Ecclesiastes 8:6 (NKJV) "...for every matter there is a time and judgment..."

May 11, 2012

We had lunch with Aunt Milla today at the Concord Villa Inn. She was here for Mom's funeral. Very sweet lady. We had a good day.

Children live what they learn. Precious in His sight and precious to me are my children.

May 24, 2012—3:55 a.m.

No one else is awake except me. I needed to talk to God.

Thank you, precious Holy, living God for saving me from me! This is the first night of a long sickness that I was able to sleep in our bed with my husband. I had acute bronchitis. They originally thought it was pneumonia and admitted me to Rancocas Valley Hospital, Lady of Lourdes, in Willingboro, NJ. Their diagnosis was wrong, but none of that matters now. I was so sick I felt like I was underwater and had to sleep in a recliner/chair for almost two weeks. First time in our bed tonight, thank You, Jesus. It felt so good to lay down flat. I'm finally getting well again.

I believe the main reason I was in the hospital was definitely a divine appointment because the sweet lady in my room was already my age exactly, sixty-four until June 9, and was from Tiberius, Africa. She was in for bad pain and gallbladder removal. I never spoke to her until they were wheeling her out to the operating room on the stretcher. She grabbed for my hand, and I reached out mine and said to her,

"I will pray for you, sweetheart."

She said, "Thank you so much."

It was then I knew I was there for a reason. God is so good! When she came back from surgery, I was there, and she was sleeping. Then they told me I could go home. I got ready to leave and went over to her bed, she pulled her hand from under the blankets and reached for mine. I held her hand and prayed for her healing, and her strength to return, as well that she would have no complications from surgery. All the glory to God, they were His words, not mine. Then I left to go home. Every time I pray, including tonight, she is in my prayers. May God continue to bless her with healing. I may never know her name or she mine, but we are sisters.

I called the ambulance that next night to take me back to the ER. I couldn't breathe and was getting much worse. Billy was angry with me, but I needed to have oxygen on the way there. When I arrived, I prayed for an angel, for God to please send me an angel. I fell asleep sitting up on the bed. A male voice woke me, calling my name. He walked in my room and said,

"Mrs. Ortiz, your diagnosis was wrong. You don't have pneumonia; you have acute bronchitis. We are sending you home with steroids called Prednisone."

I was so happy I cried and thanked God. But he wasn't my angel. This beautiful lady was sent from the Chaplin's office to me to pray. She was Catholic, but when she prayed, I knew she was my sister in Christ. The prayer she prayed over me was one of the most beautiful prayers I have ever heard—Another divine appointment. She told me she was going to stay home that night because she was tired, but something, someone, told her to go to the ER. God wanted her there for me. She was my angel.

It's 4:23 a.m. I am sleepy. Back to bed till next time. I love You, Lord, and how you work in my life is always perfect.

May 23, 2012, Saturday—5:00 a.m.

Joan died yesterday at 10:10 a.m. She was Deborah, Tom, David, and Marion's birth mom. It's a shame, but they all said, "Oh well." I wonder how they feel in their hearts. I know the pain of them being abandoned by her when they were small. It was so tragic. I do know you never, never get over that. But Jesus does fill the void if you let Him. That is between them and God, so I will let it be.

It's Joan's loss and my gain because they are each special to me in different ways. They will always be my children, not hers—especially MY Deborah. She has always been there for me. Deborah is also a fruit cake, that is one of the reasons I love her so much. God has truly blessed me with all seven of my kids and all twenty grandchildren. What a mighty blessing. Ronald, Candy, James, Deborah, Tom, David, and Marion. May my Lord and Savior Jesus Christ continue to bless them and their children as well until He takes us home. Each one is so special and so different, but I love them all the same.

If I had written and composed my own life, it wouldn't have been so wonderfully blessed as it has been. God has always been faithful and merciful, and His word is true. Such a love He has for us to give His only Son. There is nothing compared to what you have done for me, Lord. So, I give You my life every day and my heart and all I possess. Take my life and use me to Your glory, until my days here on earth are over. Your will be done, not mine. I'm indebted to You. I love You.

Your loving child and servant, Naomi.

June 9, 2012, My Birthday!

Precious Jesus, thank you for caring for me all these sixty-five years. Today is my birthday. The one You chose for me to come to this planet earth to live. I love You for always being there for me and for loving me first when I was still in my old sin. Thank You that I belong to You.

No matter when my heart stops beating, I know beyond a shadow of a doubt that I will be with You. Thank you for early this morning, Candy called and sang to me. It meant so much to hear her sing and then say I love you that I cried. Then Michael called from England. After that call was Ginny, and so far, it's only 9:00 a.m. Praise Your holy name for You always were there for me, even when I wasn't there for You. I'll always love You and sing your praises for whatever time you have given me to live on this earth, and then in heaven forever at your feet.

Billy took me to Casona to eat last night, and the food was delicious. You made a way for us to pay the bill. I sold one of my mom's rings for $110, and the bill was $109.84. If that was not Your blessing, I'll eat my hat! Hahaha, Lord, You are good all the time. I know this whole day is going to be a special blessing because of how You love me.

June 10, 2012

Another lovely birthday came and gone. As usual, the same people made my day wonderful. Jesus, Candy, Ronald, Isaac, Deborah, Tom, and Ginny. There were others that broke my heart.

June 28, 2012

The good times far exceed the bad ones. Thanks be to God, tonight we visited Ronald and the kids. Isaac was asking me a lot of questions about death and God and Jesus. He said he wanted to ask Jesus to come into his heart tonight when he says his prayers. Praise God! I hope Ronald remembers, and Isaac doesn't fall asleep. We left very late. I should have prayed with him myself. Now I wish I had.

More good news, James called and told me that he doesn't need a biopsy of whatever is in his lungs. They have it stabilized. Thank you, Jesus!

I need to catch up on writing from weeks ago on a Sunday. God spoke to my heart, Wonderful Savior, about a lady I had been praying for named Annette. Her mom had also just passed away, but she wasn't able to cope. That particular Sunday, she had asked God to send her a special message. So unbeknownst to me, Jesus told me to put a special card in an envelope and take it to her. Also, the *Daily Bread* for that day was about giving, which was in no way a coincidence, so I gave her that also. She came to me after service was over and told me that what I had given her was her answer from God that she prayed for. Isn't the Holy Spirit wonderful? If we only take time to spend time on our knees, He will speak to our hearts.

Song:

Wonderful, wonderful Jesus is to me.
Counselor, Prince of Peace, Mighty God is He.
Saving me, keeping me from all sin and shame.
Wonderful is my Redeemer, Praise His name!
("Wonderful, Jesus Is to Me
by Haldor Lillenas, 1924" 2020)

June 28, 2012

The best news in my WHOLE book!
Isaac asked Jesus to be his personal Savior and come into his heart! Praise the Lord for He is good. He prayed while saying his evening prayers with Ronald, my son, his dad. He will be six in September.

June 29, 2012

This has been a very strange week. Mom's house finally sold, but for peanuts. There was a massacre in a movie theater in Colorado, over sixty people were shot, and twelve died. They were all watching the midnight showing of the new Batman movie.

West Nile virus is becoming a serious problem, so they are spraying mosquito spray from helicopters over Willingboro and probably here also. The crops are all dying from no rain, and prices are soaring through the roof. Boats can't get to us with food because the rivers are too low, and they are going aground.

Joy and Holly are not speaking to me. Read Revelations in the Holy Bible, and you will find out why. Jesus is coming any day, praise God! It can't be soon enough for me.

Ginny tried to fight Verizon and lost and almost died trying.

All things are well on the home front, though, thank God. "All things work together for good for those who love God" (Romans 8:28 NKJV).

Holly is being evicted on July 30, 2012, and probably arrested for a bad check she wrote.

Bart and Lorraine go up and get Isaac and feed him. He and Joshua are always hungry. It is a shame that the children have to suffer so that Holly can live her crooked life. I still pray for them. I am falling asleep now; it's very late. Got to go to bed. Love You, Lord. Good night.

August 3, 2012, Friday

You'll never know how much the words "'totally clean" mean to me unless you've had cancer. I don't even like the word. It usually means a death sentence. But with God as my Savior, Healer, and Lord, we can be victorious in all things.

It doesn't mean that to me. It means that it's just another hurdle that God, Himself, is taking me over, so I stay connected to Him. He can use all our experiences to help others go through their light afflictions of the righteous, but He delivers us out of them all (Psalm 34:19). Also, I am not going anywhere until it's God's appointed time to take me, then and only then, praise God, I will be with Him forever.

Boy, isn't that true!

August 6, 2012

About two months ago, a huge blessing came from God. Danny and Billy did a morning job and took away a lady's 11X14 storage area, and they were to trash it. However, they brought it to Candy's house. What a blessing. Everything in it was brand new—clothing, shoes, slippers, and pocketbooks. All with the price tags still on them, believe it or not. Everything was either my size or Candy's size. There were even men's new shirts and shorts that were Billy's size. God is so good. He always supplies all our needs according to His riches in glory (Philippians 4:19). Jesus never fails.

August 9, 2012

I found Isaac's special, favorite brown monkey under my quilt rack. There was no mouth on it, so I drew one with a permanent marker. He came over yesterday to visit with Ronald. They arrived before me, and then I got here. He was crying, and I said, "What's wrong?"

He said, "Someone drew on my monkey!"

I never thought it would upset him. It wasn't funny to him, but to Ronald and Candy, it was hilarious.

I went to the "Route 130" diner two days ago and got a half-grilled cheese and cup of soup. A young man came in and sat at the table next to me and ordered a grilled cheese and fries. He wanted a whole one, but the waitress couldn't speak English. When his food came out, he had a half sandwich, just like mine. He looked at it very strangely and said, "Where is my other half?" You had to be there. It was so funny.

Billy watches a stupid show on TV called Splash Down. The host said he whittled a large piece of driftwood into a tiny piece of driftwood.

Angel asked me to send her one of Mom's paintings. I sent her the rose and the wine bottle with wine glasses; both had no frames. The man at the post office said, "For $34.95, it will be there on Tuesday."

I said, "I can't afford that, and I don't care if it doesn't arrive until next Christmas."

Then he said, "$7.00."

My what a big change in price! They must be crazy.

September 3, 2012, Monday, Labor Day

Precious Holy Savior, thank you for this new day. The house is quiet, and I am alone with You—No noise or distractions. Thank you for all Your mercies that are new every morning (Lamentations 3:23). Thank you for answered prayers, especially this week—all the marvelous things you've done for my family and me.

Billy's church paid Ronald and Bethany's P.S.E and G bill. Danny helped them with $75.00 first.

Ronald and Bethany's twins, Alexis and Savannah got into pre-kindergarten for free when the township wanted $5,000 first. God is so good. Then Isaac and the twins were on different schedules, and Jesus took care of that also. The principal of the school called and asked Ronald if he wanted all three on the p.m. schedule, and of course, he said yes. God gave us so much overtime at Billy's work that we were able to help Ronald and Bethany pay the $100 application fee for the twin's school. And even help Caitlyn get her school shoes.

We also paid bills that had been in the bill-drawer for months. Thank you, Jesus, I love You. The best answer to my prayers was the restoration of some of God"s spiritual gifts to me—especially the one of interpretation of tongues. The last three Sundays in a row, He gave me the word from someone who was speaking out in tongues. I remembered yesterday, God said to me, The steps of a good man are ordered by me. "Ask and ye shall receive, seek and ye shall find, knock and it shall be opened unto you" (Psalm 37:23; Matthew 7:7 KJV).

He always uses His written or spoken Word to speak to me. I can barely stand; when the anointing falls on me, it is so strong. John 10:27 says, My sheep know me, and they hear my voice. The 23rd Psalm says,

> *The Lord is my Shepherd, I shall not want. He maketh me to lay down in green pastures: he leadeth me beside the still waters. He restoreth my soul: he leadeth me in the paths of righteousness for his name's sake. Yea though I walk through the valley of the shadow of death, I will fear no evil: for thou art with me; thy rod and thy staff, they*

comfort me. Thou preparest a table before me in the presence of mine enemies: thou anointest my head with oil; my cup runneth over. Surely goodness and mercy shall follow me all the days of my life, and I will dwell in the house of the LORD for ever.

(KJV)

Amen.

There was a funny statement on the Chick-Fa-La sign today, "All children who are unattended will be given a cappuccino and a free puppy." There was also a funny quote on a tire cover on the back of a blazer, "If you get too close, I will flick a booger on you."

I just remembered, on Friday, we took Ginny to the Golden Corral for her eighty-third Birthday. The workers got together to sing happy birthday to her and asked her if she wanted the short version or the long version. She said the shortest version possible. So, they all got down on their knees, so they were short (ha-ha) and sang it!

This month Isaac will be six, and Caitlyn will be fifteen; boy does time fly!

September 8, 2012, Saturday—6:33 a.m.

Job 37:16 is what I am reading this morning—Looking at the heavens and the beautiful clouds, my life seems so insignificant. The vastness of God's universe compared to my life seems like a grain of sand in a vast desert. And yet He cares about me and even the desires of my heart. What a magnificent God! Thank you, Lord seems so little of words for the awesome gift of a new day. Here are just a few of His most recent blessings.

Pastor Scramolie called me on Tuesday morning to tell me that someone had given us $100. Praise His name, the name of Jesus!

Also, Caitlyn's test for her brain and head came out a good report. Oh, how He loves us.

I met a new lady at Home Depot that told me a wonderful story of how God blessed her son. He was flying from Florida to New Jersey to find work, so he could support his wife and four kids when a total stranger handed him $300 on the plane.

I am praying that Dianne and her hubby will eventually come to Lighthouse to worship, and if they are not saved, God will save their souls before He returns to take us home.

Dianne's husband goes to a club meeting, for people who believe in extra-terrestrials. I am very interested in attending, but I don't want to go with a total stranger, especially a man. It is pretty far from home too.

Job 37:16 (NKJV), "Do you know how the clouds are balanced? Those wondrous works of Him who is perfect in knowledge?"

The whole armor of God:

1. Truth
2. Righteousness
3. Peace
4. Faith
5. Salvation
6. The Word
7. Prayer

Seven is God's number of completions.

September 26, 2012

How to walk and talk with Jesus has been the most important thing I had learned about life by the time I had reached my middle age. There is nothing more important. If anyone reading this book should gain any wisdom at all, it should be that one thing.

Dear Lord, Precious Savior, thank you for another day in your beautiful world. Yesterday Cynthia and I went to the Beacons at Lighthouse Tabernacle Church, which is an over fifty group that meets. I was asked to lead praise and worship ten minutes before they started. Funny thing is last night, Monday evening, Jesus was talking to me about what songs to choose, and I didn't' listen or even write them down because I thought it wasn't my turn to lead. Stupid me! Again, I have the mighty God of all creation taking time to speak to my heart, and I don't even listen. I should have learned my lesson by now. You'd think if I am sixty-five and still learning the hard way, only because it still amazes me that my savior and king, Jesus, who is the creator of all I survey, would take the time to talk to a grain of sand in a vast ocean of people, little 'ole me. But He does, and He cares.

Looking back at my entire life, I see how Jesus always cared about the desires of my heart. There were many rough times. For those times, He carried me and kept me hidden from the destroyer. Thank you, Lord, for saving me over and over again. Thank you for saving me from me—When I've made plenty of wrong decisions, and you made them right. Thank you for my wonderful children and grandchildren. You have truly blessed me! My whole life has been a blessing because You love me. I can't figure out how anyone makes it through this life without Jesus. Thank you for never leaving me or forsaking me. Thank you for supplying all my needs according to Your riches in glory. Thank you for teaching me to love and forgive, even though my flesh doesn't want to. Forgive me for not spending quality time just listening to You talk to me. I would have known I was leading worship at the Beacons if I had listened.

Please hear my heart, for there are no human words to tell You of my love. So, listen to my heart. Thank you for the joy of knowing You as my savior. Thank you that Your joy is my strength.

Billy's alarm will be going off for work any minute now. Please, Lord, stay by me today, close by me. I need You more than anyone or anything. Father in Heaven, your purpose for me is like buried treasure. Each step in life I take uncovers more of the mysteries and exciting blessings You have set out for me. You have prepared a table in the presence of my enemies. You have anointed my head with oil. My cup runneth over. Surely goodness and mercy shall follow me all the days of my life, and I will dwell in the house of my Lord forever. That is what the 23rd Psalm says. The Lord is my Shepherd; I shall not want. He maketh me to lie down in green pastures. He leadeth me beside still waters. He restoreth my soul. Praise the Lord!

God is love, and love never fails.

THEN...THERE WAS LIGHT

September 30, 2012, Sunday—1:43 a.m.

Heaven and earth may pass away, but Jesus never fails (Matthew 24:35). Once again, God has heard my cry and blessed me with enough to meet an extra need. He used someone I never see except at High School reunions to meet that need—Nancy Lowe. She sent us money that we needed to get Billy's van fixed. His ways are definitely not my ways, thank God!

Billy's van was making a loud noise from the front tires. We took it to Firestone for repair. The dummies then said it was the transmission. So, we took it to Mac's at Atpro, who said they were crazy. It was the front wheel bearings. He replaced them and charged us $385.00. Of course, we never have that kind of money just laying around. We would have, but all Billy's overtime went to helping Ronald, Bethany, and Candy. So once again, I had to go to my daddy, Father God, for help. I also applied to Lighthouse Tabernacle for help from their benevolence fund and was denied. It hurt me to be denied, but I need to remember, they are only people like me. God had His plan to help me all along. It took longer, but it finally came.

As usual, last Sunday, Pastor Lexall preached on patience. Nasty word! God blessed us just at the last minute with exactly $385. I was insulted by John O'Neil by him calling me on the phone and telling me I must have assumed the church was going to help us. I told him I did not assume that. I took money from our rent to pay for Billy's van because I know my Lord and Savior. In sixty-five years, He has never let me down, and His word says, He will never see his children begging for bread (Psalm 37:25). Praise my God! Once again, He has come through at the last minute—Using a person, I haven't seen in many years to help us. And not only did the van get fixed, but the ABS light that was on for three to four years was now off too. Wonderful grace that Jesus provides, it's greater than all my sin. How shall His praise begin? Taking away my burdens, setting my spirit free, for the wonderful grace of Jesus reaches me. ("Wonderful Grace of Jesus by Haldor Lillenas, 1918" n.d.)

I have had a few surgeries. One was for the removal of a cancerous lump in my right breast. I have had two tubal ligations. There was a bleeding cyst on my ovary, and my appendix was taken out. I have had three hernia surgeries and one lithotripsy for kidney stones. I have had three miscarriages, I have had three abortions, and now I know it's murder and am so sorry for this afterward, but Jesus has forgiven me. I had one broken collar bone, a broken arm. I have had three beautiful children. So that would be nineteen surgeries in total.

THEN...THERE WAS LIGHT

I never needed pain medications or Morphine. I never had pain except before the operations. Actually, pain is a blessing. We would never know we needed help without pain.

I have had a mid-life crisis; it was when Ronald Johnson Sr. deserted us. I wanted to die. It was worse than when my husband, Frank, died of cancer. I knew where he was, in heaven, and we knew for years he was going to die. But when Ronald, Sr. left us, it was a horrible shock. It's been over twenty years, and God brought me through, as usual. It was very difficult, but I learned a lot about leaning on the everlasting arms of God. As well as several other good lessons. Praise His name. It's 2:22 a.m. I am sleepy—good night, precious Savior. If I should die before I wake, I pray my Lord, my soul to take. ("Nursery Rhyme, Thomas Fleet, 1737" 2020)

My values, goals, and priorities revolved around God and His word. Because He was all I had after Ronald Sr. left us.'

New Song:

Lift me up when I am weak
Your arms wrap around me
Your love catches me, so I'm letting go

You lift me up when I can't see
Your heart is all that I need
Your love carries me, so I'm letting go.
                    ("Lift Me Up Lyrics" 2020)

I need a big hug today, but there is no one here to hug me. Even when Billy is home, he doesn't comfort me when I cry and never hugs me—except if I ask. But that seems like a chore. I wish I had someone to hug—Someone who loves me.

The most significant realization I came to in my middle years was you can't accomplish anything worthwhile without Jesus. And life is not worth living without living for Him.

October 9, 2012,—10:10 a.m.

I can't even begin to find the words to tell you how marvelous my God is or to thank Him for being so loving, kind, and merciful. Like the Good Father, He is... so giving. Sometimes I think He even spoils us, me especially given what He did last night. Ginny gave us $100 to get us through until payday. We gave it to Ronald, Jr. and Bethany for food for the kids. Then Ginny's car broke down right by our apartment. She called us and asked for help. Billy went right out and picked her up and took her to Burlington to go bowling. She is eighty-three, and by the grace of our loving God, still bowls. Someone dropped her off here at 9:00 p.m. Billy drove her car home, and she rode with me. He got it all the way home without any trouble. Then Ginny put something in his hand for gas. He didn't even want to take it because she is so good to us. When he got in the van with me, we looked at the bill, and it was another $100. Our jaws dropped to the ground. I wanted to cry. God is so good to us. He used Ginny to bless us again, but all the glory goes to Him—without Him blessing her, she couldn't bless us. It was also His Holy Spirit speaking to her about us. Praise the Lord, God of Hosts. Glory to His name.

The best part of being middle-aged is my relationship with Jesus Christ. Just recently, I had a scope done in my urologist's office and got a wonderful report. All is well! The morning before the procedure, I was in a lot of anxiety and fear. I turned on K-LOVE radio station, and don't you know the lady on the air was talking about fear. Isn't God good? Always! I called the station and was blessed by the lady who answered, and she said I blessed her also. What that really was, was our heavenly Father blessing us both. What a wonderful daddy.

I wish God would grant me the gift of eloquent speech that John-Boy Walton had in his writings about Walton's Mountain. I could do justice to all God's blessings in my life and my children's lives and grandchildren's lives too. It seems like there are never enough human words to describe our magnificent Father God. I will still try to.

Ronald and Bethany have a kitty cat. He is really big, fat, and slow. Last week Alexis stepped on his stomach, and he wasn't breathing right. Ronald called me on the way to the veterinarian hospital to talk to me about it. I prayed that nothing would be wrong with the kitty and that God would bless Ronald. I knew they had no money to pay for any procedure on the cat. He called me on the way home to tell me how God blessed them. First, the vet told him they wanted $1500 to drain his lungs. Then they wanted $500. When they found out Ronald had no money, they changed their story to allow him and his cat to go home, and all would be well. They made him sign a note for the IV and told him that his cat's lungs were filled with blood that would slowly drain and dry, and he would be fine. When they arrived home, the cat started to eat. He was already getting well. I think the vet will take any amount of money you have. What a scam, but what a God.

November 8, 2012

Once again, faithful Father God held us in His hands, while hurricane Sandy ripped through the whole East Coast, especially New Jersey. Billy and I went to the Fountain of Life Church, which was one of the three listed shelters by the Red Cross. We had a cot and packaged army food, which had 1200 mg of salt! But it was food and shelter. Candy and Danny lost all their gas and electricity for about a week. Candy and Caitlyn slept on our floor after we got back home for three or four days. Then God restored their electricity, and they went home. The Holy Spirit gave me a word just before the storm hit. He said, "1,000 will fall at your left side, and 10,000 will fall at your right, but you will not be moved." Praise the Lord. Hundreds of people are underwater and still without power, but our family and we are all safe. Thanks be to God for His unspeakable mercies that are new every morning (Lamentations 3:23).

Every once in a while, God gives you special tiny presents that are so beautiful that you treasure them forever, like His rainbow—except that isn't tiny. I am talking about the things my grandchildren give me. I cherish every one of their gifts. Isaac made an inchworm. He said it was a caterpillar. He made it in his Pioneer class out of a clip on clothespin and four red puffballs, with one black puffball. He gave it to me, and I clipped it on my bedroom lampshade. When I go to sleep at night, I see it and remember how beautiful children are and how they have the heart of God. Caitlyn bought me a pink breast cancer pin for my jacket at her school. Just for her to think of me made my heart jump for joy.

My mother had a favorite joke about the golden years she liked to tell, and she must have told it about a million times. These two people were ninety years old and got married. They spent their honeymoon trying to get out of the car. Ha Ha... Ha Ha! I've heard it so much; it's no longer funny.

November 22, 2012, Thanksgiving Day—6:24 a.m.

Every day should be a day of giving thanks to God. We are spoiled children. He has given us everything. We lack for nothing. He is a wonderful giving Father who doesn't withhold any good thing (Psalm 84:11). The best part is He knows what is best for us, and His will for our lives is better than what we think we need. The gift of Salvation is number one on my list. I don't know about you, but I would not give my only son's life for anyone. God destroyed sin and death when He made

His ultimate sacrifice of Jesus. By the way, the best definition of real love is sacrifice.

Have you lost loved ones? Yes, many loved ones. Mom just this past May and Dad and Todd, my baby brother and Lisa, my best friend, and Frank, my kid's father, way back in May of 1980. It hasn't affected me as bad as the world grieves because I know beyond a shadow of any doubt, that they are all in Heaven with Jesus. I know someday soon, and very soon, I will be with them all again in a great reunion. By soon, I don't mean the earthly version. I mean what the Bible says when it says, our life is a vapor (John 4:14). And we will spend eternity with God in heaven, which is our real home. We are only sojourners here traveling through. Praise God.

I feel I have remained healthy in my golden years, thank God. I've had several operations, but through it all, God was there and brought me out. I'm sixty-five and still not all gray, and I am not wrinkled either. Every day I am able to drive and run errands and take care of my household, by the grace of God. Right now, I have a calcification in my uterus, which is causing me pain when I sit for long periods of time. I'm praying for a miracle, not to have any more operations. I will let you know what God does. Whatever it is going to be, I'm sure He will do His best and do what is best for me.

The best part about being a senior citizen is my grandchildren. I have two favorites, sorry, the only reason I do is that they grew up in my house. Isaac and Caitlyn. When a child grows up in your house, and you are with them every day, they become like your own. Your love them just like your own kids. Now, I know why my mom's favorite was William, she couldn't help it. He grew up in her house and became like her own kid. My children, I love them all the same. Everyone is special in their own way.

I have a special miracle. We were all praying for a check of Ronald's and Bethany's that seemed to be lost. When they finally got it in the mail, it was Veterans Day, and no one received mail that day. That just had to be God! Someone must have gotten it by mistake. It was the grace of God that they didn't trash it but had the courtesy to deliver it to Ronald. Only God can make someone do the right things in life.

Also, other answers to prayer are that Caitlyn went off all her medications without any withdrawal symptoms. Still praying for her total healing. Also, for the first time in our marriage, Billy sat down and talked to me after twelve years.

Deborah was given a new house from the Fire Company in Lampasas because they needed her land to expand. Her new house is ten times nicer than her previous home; God has really blessed her.

Song:
He was wounded for our transgressing
He was bruised for our iniquities
Surely, He bore our sorrows and
By His strips we are healed.
   ("The Healer by Lois Irwin, 1955" n.d.)

I don't think I have ever been discriminated against or treated unfairly because of my age. I have been discriminated against for being a Radle, a woman, and especially for being a Christian.

Everyone needs a good laugh, so here's one on me. About a week ago, I went to Walmart for some groceries. I had to use the bathroom and accidentally went into the men's room. Just as I was entering the handicap stall in the back, a man came in. I turned and looked at him and said, "I'm sorry, Sir, but you are in the lady's room." He knew he wasn't but didn't say one word. He was very kind and respectful! So, he waited outside the door. But two other men came in behind him. One said, "I can wait." The guy who had just come in said: "You have to wait, there is a lady in there." I heard that and said, "That's ok. I'm behind the stall; they can come in."

So, when I left, the three men were using the urinals with their backs towards me. As I passed, I said, "I'm not looking." And one man said, "That's ok we are all adults." I said, "I know, that is the problem." By the way, the first man was about 6'5" tall with long dreadlocks, light-skinned black man. I remembered him from working in Pathmark. Several minutes later, I spotted him and his wife shopping. He turned to me and said, "Look, here is my bathroom buddy." Candy wrote the whole story and put it on Facebook. Angel said, "That sounds just like you, Grandma."

November 28, 2012

My dear sweet Savior, how can anyone with half a brain say there is no God? I see You everywhere I go in everything I see. What a wonderful gift of sight you have blessed me with. I see you in the clouds and the sky, in every raindrop and every snowflake. I see you in Your beautiful rainbow. My favorite of all things—I see You in the faces of my grandchildren. I see You in the majestic waves of the branches and leaves of a beautiful tree, especially in autumn, when they begin to die. In the crushing waves of an ocean—even in a storm, I see and hear Your eminence power.

THEN...THERE WAS LIGHT

When my children were born, I saw You in each one of their perfect pink faces and smiles and hands and feet. I see You in the smiles of total strangers, especially if I smile at them first. I feel You when I pray and hear Your commanding but gentle voice speaking to my heart. I see, hear, and feel You in Your Holy Word. I taste your goodness in the special food You have provided, by Your hands, for our table. I feel Your love and mercy in every part of my life in this world. Because of You, my children have never gone without anything—ever or me either. You spoil us with the richness of this world. But I am thankful for Your love the most.

I feel You when all is still, in the night, and You are holding me, sometimes in pain, sometimes in sorrow, but You are always there. I feel my heart beating because it is Your will that for this brief time, I am alive. I've seen Your awesome power when You grew a new liver in Michaeline's mom and when You healed Malik. In every answered prayer, I feel Your presence. All the operations I've endured were because You were always there. It's because You were there that I never needed pain medications to recover. I always recuperated quickly, and You taught me to be very grateful—for the good days and the health You have blessed me with, I am grateful.

Jesus is everywhere; all you have to do is open your eyes, ears, mind, and heart to the glorious wonders of this temporary home. Be thankful and glad that this is only a breath. What God has prepared for us is our real home in Heaven for all eternity. No operations, no pain, no sorrow, no ugliness, and no enemy will be there. He has been defeated because of the blood of Jesus Christ at Calvary. Glory to God for making a way for a sinner like me to be saved by His mercy and grace. What a wonderful God we serve. Amen.

> *For to me to live is Christ, and to die is gain.*
> (Philippians 1:21 KJV)

> *And they overcame him by the blood of the Lamb, and by the word of their testimony; and they loved not their lives unto death.*
> (Revelation 12:11 KJV)

December 18, 2012

Yesterday Isaac had his Christmas show at school. He is in kindergarten, and his teacher's name is Mrs. Dee. I had to babysit for Ronald so he could see the show. Then he came home and said there was a second one, at 2:00 p.m. and I had just enough time to get there. Isaac's room came out first. I stood up and waved so he would see me. He finally found me and got a smile from ear to ear. I saw him tell his friend next to him, "That's my nanny." He waved, and the class started to sing. It was wonderful to watch and hear. At that young age, they are all so cute. Each child had small bells on both hands. They rang them as they sang. They only did two songs, then they came down the bleachers and off the stage. When Isaac got close to where I sat, he said, "I love you, Nanny." It melts my heart. I said, "I love you too." Then I left and went to lunch—what a perfect day. Thanks be to God for His unspeakable gift of Jesus.

There are some special answers to prayer I want to mention. You may think this is stupid, but I asked God to allow me to find the $11.00 framed Christmas cards in the Goodwill again because we had no extra money. He answered my prayers, I found two beautiful boxes for $.99 each, and they had a blue sticker on them, which meant on that day only, they were half price. So, I got them for $.49 each. Framed means for photos.

My Volkswagen was all done for free. The tire light was on, and the anti-freeze fluid light was on too. Volkswagen did them both as a courtesy and even washed my bug.

We just got our new lease for our apartment for 2013. They only raised our rent $10, which is another answer to prayer.

Ronald and Bethany's twins, Savannah and Alexis, were being transferred to Isaac's school in January 2013. Praise God!

Almost an Accident

About four days ago it was raining all day, and I had to go out in the evening, which I never do. The roads were still wet, and I was on Route 130, coming to the jug handle, across from the WaWa that leads home, when the car in front of me stopped dead. I tried to stop but kept sliding on the wet roads. I was about one foot away from hitting the car in front of me when I turned the wheel, or God did, to the left, and missed the car by six inches! Praise God!

December 29, 2012

Almost a new year of 2013. Where does the time go? Like God's word says, our lives are a vapor (Psalm 84:11). We are here today, gone tomorrow. The doctors are sending me for another operation on January 11, 2013. It's called a D and C, which is where they scrape the uterus. It seems to be too thick, and I've been having pain on and off pretty regular. It's like a downward pressure or pain and seems to be getting worse. They found a calcium deposit, which the doctor told me is not causing my pain. But I know that my Savior, Jesus Christ knows, and He cares, and right now He is carrying me, I am sure. I am a little concerned, but deep down, I know my Lord has everything planned from my conception and birth to my going home to Him. Therefore, I need not worry.

Special Prayer Note:

While I was praying a few weeks ago, I asked God if He made a cure, a natural cure, for cancer, and He said, "yes". He said one word only—"Thistle". I had no idea what that was, so I called my nearest health food store, and she read to me the benefits of Milk Thistle, and also of Holy or Blessed Thistle. Both of those are natural plants. I almost couldn't believe what she read to me. Also, her store, Lois' Health Food Cupboard, sell them both. The Milk Thistle is very beneficial in lots of health problems, and cancer is one of them. I wonder why no one knows about it. In my heart, I know that God made a natural cure for everything that ails us, which is why I asked. Now I just have to figure out what to do.

The song in my heart today is *Great Is Thy Faithfulness*.

Great is they faithfulness, oh God my Father,
There is no shadow of turning with thee.
Thou changest not, thy compassions they fail not.
As thou hast been, thou forever will be.
(chorus)
Great is thy faithfulness,
Great is thy faithfulness,
Morning by morning, new mercies I see.
All I have needed thy hath provided.
Great is thy faithfulness, Lord unto me.
Verse 3:
Pardon for sin and peace that endureth,
Thine own dear presence to cheer and to guide.
Strength for today and bright hope for tomorrow.
Blessings all mine, with ten thousand beside.

("Great Is Thy Faithfulness
by Thomas O. Chisholm, 1923" n.d.)

AMEN!

I almost forgot, last Sunday, Pastor Scramolie came up to me in the a.m. service at Lighthouse Tabernacle and told me that someone gave them $100 for me for Christmas. I started to cry, to think that God is always reminding me how faithful He is and how He cares about the desires of our hearts. Praise the Lord, for He is good. His mercies endureth through all generations (Lamentations 3:23).

God...does great things, which we cannot comprehend. "For He says to the snow, 'Fall on the earth'" (Job 37:5–6 NKJV).

CHAPTER 4

January 18, 2013

    This is what I wish for, snow. But also, we never get any snow. It's almost a thing of the past. I haven't seen a good snow for years in our area. But when I was little, the snow came up to my waist or higher. We played in it every day for weeks. It was cold enough for the creek right by our house to freeze over solid enough that we could ice skate on it. The snow was also clean enough to eat.
    I've been sick for about two to three weeks with a horrible cough and mucus throat. I've been on Methyl Prednisone and Cipro Floxin, and I am done with medications and still sick. I am much better than I was. Ronald and Bethany asked me to babysit for them. It's a Friday night, and I wanted to go to bed early, but I know how desperate Ronald is to get a break from all

those kids. His friend Billy gives him money to gamble with in Atlantic City almost every week. He always wins; only one time did he lose. This time Bethany wanted to go with him, so I said yes.

> *There is a saying that goes like this:*
> *Prejudice is a burden that confuses*
> *the past, threatens the future*
> *and renders the present inaccessible.*
> ("Quote by Maya Angelou" n.d.)

I have to say, it's not a burden, it's a sin. When you think anyone lesser of a human being than yourself, you elevate yourself above them and become better than them in your own eyes. God's word says, He created us all equal and loves us all the same (John 13:16; Acts 10:34–35; Galatians 3:28). He only hates the sin, not the sinner. He actually says, "For there is no respect of persons with God" (Romans 2:11 KJV). So, prejudice in any form is a sin.

Anyway, since I was still recuperating from illness, Ronald said Bethany would pick me up, and he would drive me home. All the kids would be asleep. Haha—never happened. There was Isaac, who is six, and the twins who are four and a half, Michael turned two on Christmas Day and Jayden, who is three months old.

Plus, there is Sukie, who Ronald also watches who is two and a half. Every day she is kept by Ronald. She comes on Monday through Friday from her daycare "Papa Bears Daycare," So, he has six kids every day. I'll never know how he does it. Except that God has given him a special grace and favor that most men do not have to be a mother hen, so to speak.

Back to the story: after Bethany picked me up, I could hear all the kids upstairs, running around, not sleeping, and it was almost 9 p.m. They knew somehow that I was there, and they were excited. Jayden was in his baby swing, and he was also wide awake. Michael was in his crib, crying. I thought to myself, *Fun, fun, fun... NOT!*

After Ronald and Bethany left with Billy, by the way, he was there when I arrived. Just waiting to leave. As soon as they left, Isaac came down and said, "Nanny, can we come down?" My heart melted, and I said, "Yes." So, he and his twin sisters came downstairs with their blankets and pillows, and we watched *Beverly Hills* on Netflix. They were good kids, and Michael stayed in his crib and eventually went to sleep. I made Jayden a bottle, and he ate it quickly and went to sleep also. After the movie, Isaac went up in his room and got his cigar box filled with stickers and gave it to me as a gift. He said, "I want you to have this because I love you." He is so precious. Ronald said they were his most prized possessions. I feel bad taking them, but Isaac gave me the best that he had. Just like Jesus, or rather God when He gave us Jesus. True love is giving of yourself to someone else, the best that you can give. The best that you have that is what love gives. No one will ever give a gift like Jesus. Praise the Lord God for His unspeakable gift. God's word says, "...and a child shall lead them" (Isaiah 6:11 KJV).

During the night, Isaac asked if he could look in my purse for my scissors to cut something. I said sure because they were kids' safety scissors. While he was looking, he found two Reese's cups, two lollypops, and Chick-Fil-A mint and ran to me and said, "Nanny, look what I found." Then after he asked if he could have them, he shared them with his sisters too. We watched a second movie, and it was called *The Lorax*, both kiddy movies and very good. After *The Lorax*, we turned the TV off and went to sleep in the living room. Jayden was still asleep in his swing.

Around midnight or a little later, I was awakened by Michael upstairs crying, so I prayed for God to help him go back to sleep. I was awake then, so I called Ronald to see if they were on their way home. He said they had won $140 and also paid Billy back, but that he picked up two of his work buddies on the way down. All three of them had gone to the club/ bar to drink and had left Ronald and Bethany alone in the casino. Ronald wanted to leave, so he went to the club to ask Bill, and he said, "1 a.m." Never happened! Somehow, I knew it wouldn't because drunks are not reliable or truthful. 2 a.m. rolled around, still no coming home. Finally, I called at 2:45 a.m. and said, "Take a cab." The cab driver said $300, so Ronald got Billy's keys and told him he was bringing Bethany home and then taking me home, then going all the way back to Atlantic City for the three drunks. Believe it or not, I prayed all night that God would keep them safe and also make another way.

By the time I got to my apartment, it was 4:30 a.m. Billy, my own Billy, was snoring and never cared where I was. Then Ronald headed back to Atlantic City for his friend Bill and the drunks. He asked me to pray for him to stay awake. I was already praying all night for God to change things. Boy did He ever! I've noticed in my brief sixty-five years on planet earth that God always answers prayers and always does far more exceedingly better than we could ever think or do. Always.

Ronald started back on 295 South and got a call from Billy. Billy told him his dad came all the way down to Atlantic City and took them home. Guess where Ronald was when he called? One the exit away from Haddonfield. Amazing how our majestic, marvelous, wonderful, matchless Father God not only answers prayers but sends us a small miracle too. Even when we are not exactly where we should be but have a good heart and mean well. Heaven and earth may pass away, but Jesus Never Fails! (Matthew 24:35).

A saying I found says:

> *Men are not superior by reason*
> *Of the accidents of race or color.*
> *They are superior who have*
> *The best heart.*
> ("Quote by Robert Green Ingersoll" n.d.)

Bull! No one is superior but our God. The men that chose to follow Him and ask Jesus to live in their hearts do not become superior to anyone, but they become one with the Master who created the universe. They have His wonderful blessings and heritage because we are children of the only, one and only true God and King, Jesus Christ.

Little Tidbits

January 20, 2012

> *For who is God, except the Lord, and who is a Rock, except our God.*
>
> (2 Samuel 22:32 NJKV)

The biggest mistake I ever made was not listening to my parents or God at an earlier age. The second biggest mistake was having a tubal ligation. However, that didn't matter to God. He blessed me with a special son named Ronald. My miracle baby! The third biggest mistake was not telling anyone that I was raped. I was sixteen, and he was 22. I think then the course of my life would have changed. I don't want anything to change or be changed. Everything in my life has been a blessing, especially my grandchildren and my children, all of them. James, David, Tom, Deborah, Candy, Ronald, and even Marion. The smartest decision I ever made was to follow Jesus, of course. Wherever He leads me, I will follow.

Now getting back to my blessings, my children, and my grandchildren. I always was angry at my mother for having favorites. Well, I understand why now, especially about the grandchildren—Mainly because they live with you or grow up in your house. Caitlyn grew up in my home, so she became my favorite. Then Isaac spent more than the whole first year of his life with me. He became my favorite also. Still to this day, Caitlyn and Isaac are both my favorites, I can't help myself.

I always loved to ice skate and loved cold weather. Everyone else would go home, but I wanted to stay and skate all night. I wish I had turned pro in ice skating, but my life was blessed in so many other ways, it didn't matter. I also always wanted to go up in a hot air balloon. Maybe I will someday still. I always wanted to go to England to meet Jenifer, Michael's sister, but I hated flying. I have a fear of both heights and flying. Taking a cruise ship would have taken forever.

I think I have a lot of spiritual gifts I haven't used yet, like painting and drawing, just like my mom. I never used the talent that God gave me for those things. I have used the talents of writing and poetry, which I just love, as well as writing and singing songs. God has given me many gifts, and one is my love of children. They are so precious and so innocent. Even when someone else's child gets hurt, it pains my heart, just like God's heart. He has given me the gift of giving and tongues, as well as the interpretations of tongues and prophecy, like knowing the future in somethings, of course not in all things, and most of all prayer. I believe intercession is a real gift of God.

I think the nicest thing I have done is leading another person in prayer to Jesus. It is also the most precious thing when someone accepts Jesus Christ as their Savior. My husband, Billy's dad, was one of them. I love talking about Jesus and telling others who are lost how marvelous a savior He is. Two weeks after he asked Jesus to be his Savior, he went to Heaven. There were a lot of others, but I can't remember the names. God knows who they are. Even if you just pray for them to be saved, God can plant a seed. Actually, He doesn't need you or me. We need Him.

There was one thing I had put off doing until it was too late, but it must have not even been that important, or I would have remembered what it was.

Precious in the sight
Of the Lord is the
Death of His saints.

(Psalm 116:15 KJV)

I did do something that many people warned me not to do, and yet I did it anyway, and that was to start smoking. God even saved me from that Thirty-one years ago, when I was carrying Ronald in my tummy. I quit, by the grace of God, and I thank Him every day for helping me and giving me His strength to quit smoking. It turned out good because God even cleaned up my lungs, isn't He wonderful?

The most important decision I have ever had to make was putting my mother in a care facility. I do feel we made the right decision after everything was done, which was between Joy, Bart, Timmy, and I. Even though in my heart I think she would have lived a lot longer than she did, still God's will for her life was done. He takes you home regardless of what someone else does when He is ready.

The incident in my life that changed everything for me was when I was raped. God made my life beautiful, anyway. He took ugly rags and turned them into gold, that was the worst. The best incident was the birth of my children and grandchildren. It was also when I married Frank and took his children to be mine. What a blessing, my kids have been to me. I wouldn't want my life any other way. God's will is perfect.

Two places I have always wanted to go are to England and a tropical island.

In life, all I have ever really wanted to be was a wife and mother. God has fulfilled every one of my dreams. If I went to Heaven today, there is nothing else I wish for or need. All I ever needed was Jesus. He has made my life complete and fulfilled all my heart's desires. I lack for nothing. All my dreams have come true!

There was one person who saved my life. It was Dianna Cross, I was drowning in a pool, and she jumped in and pulled me out, saving me.

February 9, 2013

I had a close brush with death when God sent me to Haiti. I was fifty years old, not sure of the date of the trip. He spoke to my heart every time I prayed for the team that was already going. They were a group of men and women from First Baptist Church in Mt. Holly. Every time I got down on my knees to pray, specifically for them, God's still small voice would say, "You're also going." I would look up from my bowed position and say, "No, I'm not. I'm only praying for the ones who are." The next time I prayed, God would say, "Yes, you are going." Finally, I called the church and found out the name of the team captain, who was Brian and Alice. Brian told me what God had told him that there was another woman going but not from his church. So, when I called Brian, he confirmed what I had heard God telling me. To make a long story short, I went. What an experience! I was so blind to think God was using me to change hearts when all along He wanted to change my heart.

Deborah came all the way from Texas to run my business, "Ronald's Moving & Hauling," because no one else was able to do it or knew the business like her. We were there for ten days—Once in the missionary's house in Port-A-Prince, and the jungle. I saw God do many miracles. But when I returned to the United States, I was very sick with a parasite and didn't even know until it took over my whole system.

In Haiti, the last day before we came home, I didn't know it then, but that was a parasite that has laid its eggs on me. They would later hatch and feed off my body. The intense, demonic itching was so horrific; I wanted to die! Itching is a curse, and Jesus became a curse for us on Calvary. No American doctor knew how to help me. I suffered terrible agony for six to nine months until finally, I went to see an international disease specialist. He gave me one pill that finally killed all of them. They were so terrible; I even drank medicinal turpentine that the owner Ed, of East Park Pharmacy, gave me. It was horrible... but I figured if it didn't kill them, maybe I would kill me. Thank God for his infinite mercy and wisdom and healing mercies. In His time. I learned many lessons in those 6–9 months. One was total dependence on Christ.

There is a poem that states:

Into each life
Some rain must fall,
Some days must be
Dark and dreary

("The Rainy Day by Henry Wadsworth Longfellow -" n.d.)

God's word says about this, '...He sends rain on the just and the unjust" (Matthew 5:45 NKJV). It also says, "I can do all things through Christ who strengthens me" (Romans 8:28 NKJV). The Word also says, "Many are the afflictions of the Righteous, but the Lord delivers him out of them all" (Psalm 34:19 NKJV).

February 09, 2013

Precious Savior, I started to write today about the beautiful snowfall we awoke to. But I got sidetracked by the proceeding questions from this journal book. Each tree and bush are outlined in beautiful, velvety, white snow. There never was a more beautiful Painter than God, nor a more beautiful canvas than His earth. One of His most precious gifts, for me, has to be sight, which most of us take for granted. When I awoke to this miracle of snow, I knew I had to write about God and for His beautiful handy work—How He blessed me!

One time I was hurt the most in life, I think, is when Ronald, Sr. walked out on our marriage, and our business, and our son Ronald, Jr. Besides Haiti, it was the only other time in my life that I wanted to die.

Let me tell you about all the miracles that God did in Haiti.

1. God changed my heart.
2. I learned to hear His voice and obey.
3. He healed me of that parasite.
4. Haiti made me have a new love and affection for what God has given us here in America because of the extreme poverty in that country.
5. The Caribbean Sea was right where we were. It was the most beautiful ocean I had ever seen.
6. The love those people had for Jesus was amazing. Especially considering they had nothing else, He was their everything.
7. When I saw a man trying to read his Bible in the dark, I cried.

February 13, 2013

Great is Thy faithfulness, O God, my Father.
There is no shadow of turning with thee.

Thou changest not, thy compassions, they fail not.
As thou hast been, thou forever wilt be.
Great is Thy faithfulness,
Great is Thy faithfulness.
Morning by morning, new mercies I see.
All I have needed, thy hand hath provided.
Great is Thy faithfulness, Lord unto me.
("Great Is Thy Faithfulness
by Thomas O. Chisholm, 1923" n.d.)

Great is Thy faithfulness also to my children and grandchildren. Ronald found a real nice dresser in someone's trash. It was very old and very heavy. Danny helped him lift it into his van. After he got home, he had no one to help him get it out. The worst thing was that it needed to go upstairs in Isaac's room. I prayed that God would send someone to him to help him lift it. He went out to the van to get it at 10:30 p.m., and you would think no one would even be up then. God heard my prayers and sent a man, just walking by the van to help him take it in and all the way upstairs. Wonderful Lord Jesus, always the same, never fails to answer and help. He even cares about the little things, like a dresser. Isn't He wonderful?

April 4, 2013

Precious Savior, still my refuge and my strength.

Then the trees of the woods shall rejoice before the Lord...
(1 Chronicles 16:33 NKJV)

Beautiful Lord

Your so beautiful, nothing can compare
Precious Savior, all my sin you had to bare.
Your so beautiful, nothing can compare.
Look around you, for His beauty is all there.
Every flower, tree, and rainbow
All I see is thee
Every cloud and sea and bird,
Make Your voice to be heard.

Your mercy, O Lord, is in the heavens' Your faithfulness reaches to the clouds.
(Psalm 36:5 NKJV)

Jesus

Jesus, precious, Jesus, You are my guiding light.
Jesus, precious Jesus, You hold me through the night.
Precious Holy Savior, You're there when I call.
You're always near me, Jesus, even when I fall.

You saved me, forgave me; You are my closest friend.
Jesus precious Savior, You're with me to the end.
You are my comfort, Jesus; You even save my tears.
You guide me through life's valleys and love me through my fears.

There have been times I've wondered if You were really there.
But You taught me, Holy Savior, compassion and Your care.
My Jesus precious Shepherd, please always help me see.
You hold me through life's journey; You've even carried me.
You hold me through life's journey; You've even carried me.

(Naomi Jean Radle 2011)

The happiest event in my adult life was when I asked Jesus to be my savior, and He said yes.

> *Indeed, let God be true but every man a liar. As it is written: "that you may be justified in Your words, and may overcome when You are judged."*
>
> *(Romans 3:4 NKJV)*

Life Is a Vapor

God's word, the Holy Bible, says, "life is a Vapor" like a breath on a cold day, or the steam from a pot of water (James 4:14). Here for a few brief seconds, then gone. Since I've gotten older, that is self-evident to me. It seems like just yesterday, I was playing hide and seek in my mom's front yard. It was dusk, and my two friends Andrea and Susan were with me and my sisters and brothers. Then I cried till I had no more tears left when my white, fluffy puppy Snow Ball got hit by a car and died. I played monopoly with my Best friend every day for over two weeks. The game never ended. I traded feathers with a boy in my fourth-grade class named David Wilson. Andrea and I climbed trees and made tree houses. We ate a whole jar of mayonnaise with two knives.

I held my first son James in my arms for the first time and was amazed at how wonderfully beautiful God had made him. I had never even seen anything more beautiful.

Then I turned around, and now I am old, and it was only yesterday that I was catching lightning bugs in a jar. All of God's word is true, especially, "Life is a Breath." Soon I will not be here any longer, but with my Savior and Lord Jesus Christ for all eternity.

Sometimes I can't wait to go home, and other times I love being here with my grandchildren and my family. But I do feel like I am a sojourner, traveling through this hurried life, on my way to the next. Sometimes all the mundane things I do here seems like such a waste of time—When all that really matters is what I do for others and Christ.

So, then why bother? Because this is the life we have been given and every breath we take is a gift from God, and what we do with it matters to Him.

April 4, 2013

These prayers are added today to glorify my savior and Lord, Jesus Christ. I only hope anyone who reads this will fall to their knees and ask Jesus to be their savior. Those who already know Him will have a new 'awe' and reverence for who He really is and can be in their life. Glory—all glory to God, for He is holy. Matthew 6:18 (NKJV), "So that you do not appear to men to be fasting, but to your Father who is in the secret place; and your Father who sees in secret will reward you openly."

May 12, 2013, Mother's Day

I have witnessed a seemingly supernatural event. I was getting ready for bed, and it was close to midnight on Mother's Day. I had been very sad and depressed the day before because Mom died on May 6th last year, which was also just prior to Mother's Day. Billy was already asleep when I saw a large, quick flash of bright white light in my dark hallway. There were no doors or windows or any place the light could have come from. It was only there for maybe one second. Then it was gone. I believe in spiritual happenings, just like I believe in God, Jesus, and the Holy Spirit. I think just maybe that was my guardian angel or Mom telling me she is ok, and at peace in Heaven. Or maybe I need to "listen" more. I think it is very special to have a heavenly visitation, not everyone has them, only certain people.

If I could change how I raised my children, I would actually change nothing about it. I raised them all in church and in the fear of the Lord Jesus Christ. They are all "saved" and on their way to eternal glory in Heaven.

June 9, 2013, A little after Midnight on My Sixty-six Birthday!

God is always *soooo* good to me. He never fails, and His mercies endure forever (Psalm 100:5). There is nothing on earth like His never-ending love. He surely is the greatest and only Lord, Savior, King, Lover, Friend, Physician, Provider, and all I would ever need in this life and in the next life.

Since a week ago, God has been giving me wonderful presents every day leading up to my birthday! On June 4, Candy called and gave me $100, and Ronald gave me $20 for gas and fed me lunch. Candy's was $50 for my birthday and $50 to loan for good. Deborah called in my Fingerhut account and paid my $60 bill the next day. On June 5, Pastor Scramolie called with money from the Beacons for Billy and me. That turned out to be $300. God is awesome! The next day continued blessings followed, and then Saturday, I went with Bart and Lorraine to the PA yard sales. Lots of good fun, not to mention the food. When I got home, Billy surprised me with a beautiful cross and pin set and a beautiful card. The cross and pin set was sterling silver with a gold heart over the middle. Very nice! I love it. Like I said, every day this week, God has blessed me. It felt like a week-long birthday party.

Tomorrow I'm meeting my kids and grandkids at Cassimere Restaurant for 2:00 p.m. lunch. I can't wait, I only hope James is ok enough to join us. By God's grace, he will be there.

Church in the a.m. tomorrow Sula, my new Greek friend, and she will be commissioned a "Stephens Minister." She is a helpful and wonderful sister in Christ.

Then all week, I expect God to continue His wonderful blessings. Aunt Milla is taking us to lunch on Monday for my birthday. I got birthday cards from Candy, Billy, Lorraine and Bart, Michael Kounnas, Kay and Mark, James and Ronald. Someone besides Jesus loves me. Thank you, Lord, for surrounding me with people who care about me and love me for who I am. Thank you for the best birthday ever. We may never be wealthy or money-wise, but we are rich beyond measure for our family love, and time we spend together. Almost forgot, Billy was over Ronald and Bethany's all week to help Ronald with his kids. Wonderful, wonderful, wonderful.

> *I shall be telling this with a sigh*
> *Somewhere ages and ages hence:*

> *Two roads diverged in a wood, and*
> *I took the one less traveled by,*
> *and that has made all the difference.*
> ("The Road Not Taken by Robert Frost" n.d.)

Please choose the narrow road, the one less traveled... stay close to the Bible. It says the road that leads to hell and destruction is wide. And the road that leads to God and His heaven is very narrow.

I love my life the way it is. I would not change a thing; God has carried me all these years, and His way is perfect. I have enjoyed all the periods of my life. If I had to live my life over again, I would do nothing differently. Everything was wonderful, the valleys and the mountain tops.

My prayer partner and friend Ginny, Virginia Andrews, is eighty-three and just had open-heart surgery. Unbelievable that God has kept her alive, and she is getting stronger every day. She has no family, and her husband is deceased. Every day all her neighbors get together and bring her breakfast, lunch, and dinner. God is so good. Sometimes He surrounds us with "angels," and it is even hard to imagine that this is happening in these times when everyone is lovers of self. But God is still doing miracles.

It was so nice to hear from my brother Timmy. He is a recluse; no one hears from him. But he called, and we talked for a long time. He told me about a lady at his work that won't give him the time of day. He asked me to pray, so she would talk to him. So, I did and believe it or not, the next day, she said, "Hello," and "How are you doing?" God still answers prayers. Timmy called me, delighted that they had a chance to talk.

Ronald and Bethany got their new house, glory to God! I hope they can rent to buy, and someday own the place if Jesus tarries.

July 1, 2013, Early a.m.

Dear Precious Jesus, thank you for your Holy Spirit, and all you've done for my family and me. Thank you for answering prayers. Always thank you for Your mercies that are new every morning (Lamentations 3:23). Thank you for all our provisions, that You always supply all our needs, according to Your riches in glory. Thank you for Your Word that is true and sharper than any two-edged sword. Thank you for Your healing mercies. Thank you for my children, all seven and all my grandbabies, all twenty! What a blessing they have been. Thank you for my husband, Billy, even though we rarely see eye to eye. I still love him because he loves You.

We need you today, that is an understatement, we need You more today than yesterday—Half as much as tomorrow. Candy, James, and I need healing, Your touch on our bodies. Please be merciful to us and heal us, just like You did at Calvary. Cover us with Your precious blood and confuse the schemes and plots of the enemy over our lives. In Jesus' name and for His glory.

Amen.

Jesus was born, crucified, risen, and coming again! All our lives will soon be past. Only what's done for Christ will last.

August 7, 2013

> *"Amazing love, how can it be? That my sweet Lord would die for me"*
>
> ("You Are My King
> by Billy James Foote, 2001" n.d.).

The mighty God of all creation, all we survey, all the heaven's and earth and all the universe, would create you and me because He was lonely, out of dirt, then send His only son—Jesus to die on a cruel cross, be humiliated and beaten, just so we could be forgiven of our sins, to be with Him in Heaven forever.

That is a real mystery to me. But I sure am glad He did. Also, how He loved us while we were yet sinners and wooed us like a lover so we would to come to Him. Praise the Lord, for He is more than worthy to be praised. More than just good, He is wonderful.

My values try to line up with Christ's. In God's word, it says, our body is His temple (1 Corinthians 6:19). And it belongs to Him, not to me. All I have done throughout my life when I was young and stupid to ruin it. I'd never do again, but all my sin, God has buried in the deepest sea, and He remembers it no more. Praise the Lord, for He is good!

The advice I would give about getting through difficult times and coping with change is to hold tight and never let go of God and His holy word. Every word is true, and He always, always, always makes a way of escape. "Pray without ceasing," you have not, because you ask not (1 Thessalonians 5:17; James 4:2 NKJV). Remember, God's word also says, all things happen for good, for those who love the Lord (Romans 8:28).

Jesus Loved Me

Long before the world was formed
Long before I was a babe,
Long before I heard of Calvary,

Jesus loved me and knew my name.

Long before the word Salvation,
Hit my ears and took my heart.
Long before they crucified Him,
Jesus knew we'd never part.
　　　　　(Naomi Jean Ortiz, August 8, 2013)

The Son of the living God, "Jesus," being crucified for us is the same as if we were killed for a worm because He is the great and mighty God.

And just as you want men
To do to you,
You also do to them likewise.
　　　　　　　　　(Luke 6:32 NKJV)

August 8, 2013

Good News! My mammogram came back for the fourth year in a row, clean and clear! Praise God!

More good news... Jesus never fails. "Heaven and earth can pass away," but Jesus never fails (Matthew 24:35). We had a terrific heatwave last month, the day it happened was when Ronald and Bethany's central air conditioner broke. The man sent out to repair it said it was completely dead. The owners of their home said they have no money to replace it. Sometimes it's hard to comprehend how wonderful God is. This may sound hard to believe, but no lie, Ronald sold a dryer to a man and made $50 and $25 extra to deliver it. Then the man asked him to come around the back of his home to get rid of something. It was his central air unit! The unit was still working and was totally free! The mechanic came back out and said it worked and was paid by the owner to hook it up—"Amazing love, how can it be? That my God should die for you and me" ("You Are My King by Billy James Foote, 2001" n.d.).

How Do You Feel About Abortion?

Horrible! It is murder. Plain and simple murder, there is nothing worse than killing innocent babies. Some are even killed at full birth weight, which is just unbelievable that a society that was founded on Almighty God would stray so far away as to do a horrific crime against God and human nature by allowing abortions. When I was young and very stupid, I had nine pregnancies: three living children, three spontaneous miscarriages, and three abortions. I'm very ashamed of what I have done. But God, in His infinite mercy, has forgiven me.

I believe in God's Word, and I believe it teaches that when a man takes another man's life, he is to be put to death by the state. Most murders just serve minimum time and get loose to do it again. Jesus has to be coming soon because society is so far away from the truth of God's Word today. I don't know that they wouldn't see it if it were to bite them in the butt.

August 11, 2013

> *Sweet Jesus,*
> *You are my Sonshine*
> *My only Sonshine.*
> *You make me happy,*
> *When skies are grey.*
> *You'll never know dear (Lord);*
> *How much I love you.*
> *Please don't take my sunshine away.*
> ("You Are My Sunshine –
> Original by Jimmie Davis 1940" n.d.)

—I love you with all my heart, Naomi

What Is Most Important to Making a Marriage Work?

...Both people knowing Christ Jesus as their Savior and putting Him first in everything. Also, allowing the husband to have the final say in all major decisions. Everything else should be equal and shared by both people. Most important is that a marriage is between one man and one woman. That is what the Word of God teaches.

What Is Your Advice in Divorce and Remarriage?

Again, the Bible teaches that marriage shall be a union of one man and one woman, who stay together for life. God hates divorce... but if anyone divorces, there is forgiveness and mercy from Him. I've been married four times, but only once in God's eyes. When I was sixteen, I was raped by a twenty-two-year-old man, and instead of arresting him, my parents made him and I marry—Big mistake that was. God didn't hold me responsible for that rape.

My second marriage was a true one. I was twenty. I fell for Frank E Jr. with all my heart. I divorced the rapist, and Frank and I were married. Frank died in April of 1980 of cancer. According to the Bible, I was free to marry again. I was thirty-two when I met Ronald W. Johnson Sr. and temporarily insane from the death of

Frank. We married and had Ronald Jr. He left us for another woman when I was forty-two, and Ronald Jr. was nine. I stayed alone for over ten years after that. Then I met William Ortiz and married again in December of 2000.

What Is Your Advice on Parenting?

Being loving and kind and always tell the truth. Most importantly, to take your kids to Sunday School.

What Are the Basic Principles of Your Religion?

Religion separates all of us, where the devil wants us to be. Being "born-again," saved by God's grace, is NOT a religion but a way of life. I live to the best of my ability according to what the Bible says. The Bible teaches us that you MUST be born-again to see the kingdom of Heaven. John 3:16 (KJV), "For God so loved the world that He gave His only begotten Son, that whosoever believeth on Him should not parish, but have everlasting life." Romans 10:9 (KJV), "That if thou shalt confess with thy mouth the Lord Jesus, and shalt believe in thine heart that God hath raised him from the dead, thou shalt be saved." You must:

1. Admit you are a sinner.
2. Admit you believe in Jesus and that He died for your sins.
3. Ask Jesus to forgive you and your sins and come into your heart and live. And He will.

From then on, you belong to Jesus, and He is your savior. He will change your life. I have changed my beliefs during my lifetime. Some would call it changing my religion. I grew up in a Baptist church where they taught me the fundamentals of religion. When I was old enough, God gave me the wisdom to believe there was more to this life that I had been taught. I became a believer in the Pentecostal faith. Believing in the whole Bible and not just the part to be saved. Jesus wants us to have power in our lives, and for that, He gave us the Holy Spirit to help us day by day.

For me to tell you what God means to me, is a loaded answer. First and foremost, God is everything, and He means everything to me. He is my life. I couldn't live without Him and wouldn't want to, for even a second. He is every breath I take; He is the amazement and wonder in my grandbabies' eyes. He is the beauty that surrounds me in the trees, leaves, and animals. He is the song in my heart. He is my refuge and my strength.

He is my hiding place. He is my God, my Lord, my savior, and the Love of my life.

September 3, 2013

My most favorite scripture is Mark 16:15–18,

> And He said to them, "Go into all the world and preach the gospel to every creature. He who believes and is baptized will be saved; but he who does not believe will be condemned. And these signs will follow those who believe: In My name they will cast out demons; they will speak with new tongues; they will take up serpents; and if they drink anything deadly, it will by no means hurt them; they will lay hands on the sick, and they will recover.

Praise His name in all the earth. Praise the Lord God!

If I could ask God one question, for a long time it was going to be "Why did He make men so proud and stupid, hurtful, and vain?" but then I realized when I see Jesus or God for the first time, nothing else will matter, except for being in His presence and worshiping Him. Also, I have learned Mother Anne's favorite scripture was about how we are to take the beam out of our own eye before we try to remover the splinter from my brother's eye (Matthew 5:7). Plus, whoever is without sin, cast the first stone (John 8:7) and the scripture about judge not, least ye be judged (Matthew 7:1). God knows how to put you in your place while being gentle, kind, and merciful. The bible says for us to forgive 70 X 7 times, which means always (Matthew 18:22).

Under this beautiful sunset is what Emerson thinks prayer is. But prayer is your lifeline between you and God. It is personal, necessary, intimate, friendly, reverent, but most of all, it should always be all the time. Not a time that one talks to God only when you need help, but thankful and praiseworthy.

I constantly pray, with conversation and companionship toward the love of my life. As often as I can, I talk to the Lord all day. I involve Him in every part of my life. Waking, dressing, eating, shopping, housework, driving, sleeping, even making love. I praise His name and thank Him constantly. I ask for traveling mercies for my family and me: Billy, Ronald, Candy, James, Deborah, Tom, David, and Marion and all my grandbabies. I thank Him for His mercies that are new every morning (Lamentations 3:23). I thank Him for a day without pain, and even for the pain because it draws me closer to Him. Like now, early in the morning, I'm thanking Him now for the glistening leaves that shine in His beautiful sunlight like Deborahs.

I have gotten more spiritual as I have gotten older too. I think we all acquire more wisdom with age, or should I say, we all should acquire more wisdom as we age. I'm still not a constant reader, but I love to pray and write to Jesus, my best friend, Lord, and Savior. He is my healer, my confidant, provider, and everything I need. More than ever today, His Holy Spirit has been prompting me to pray for the lost. I pray for salvation for people I know and meet every day. Even strangers, I pray they will receive salvation. I used to only pray for those that I knew, but now I pray for whoever God puts on my heart and all those around me, especially in cars on the road.

I definitely believe in angels. They are created beings by God for His messengers and to do His bidding here on earth and in Heaven. If you believe in the Bible, God's Holy Word, that is what it says angels are. I believe we all have at least one, especially children. I sometimes can feel mine on my side while I am in prayer. Wonderful Savior, He thought of everything. I know of at least three or four times my angels have saved me from terrible pain or even death. In my car, in the hospital, and even in public. God is good, all the time!

I surely and absolutely believe in miracles. I have seen several. I saw with my own eyes, my son, Ronald's legs, straighten when he was two or three years old.

His doctor told us to buy braces to straighten them. I couldn't put them on, I cried. Then I went over to Ann Johansen's (Ronald Sr.'s mom). She told me to take my hands and lay them on Ronald Jr.'s legs, and she put her hands on mine then prayed out loud while I cried and agreed. The next doctor visit Ronald had, his doctor said, "Boy, those braces did a wonderful job." I told him we took them back, and God healed my son. He just looked at me, amazed.

Our spirit man is who we really are. The flesh is just an outer suit to be able to live on this earth. Our real man is our spirit. God's word, the Bible says, "...to be absent in the body, is to be present with the Lord" (2 Corinthians 5:8 KJV). I'm looking forward to stepping out of this flesh and walking into glory with my spirit man. I'm looking forward to seeing Jesus. If people only knew that this life is a vapor or just a breath, and our spirit man lives for eternity, in either heaven or hell, they would run, not walk to the closest church to have a personal relationship with their Creator—Jesus, God, and the Holy Spirit.

I believe in the afterlife of heaven. Nothing we ever knew or saw on earth is what our afterlife will be like. There are even colors we don't have on earth there. Jesus is there, and all our families and friends who died before us. There will be a great reunion there. The light surrounding Jesus will be more than we can imagine or even look at. The peace and happiness will be no match for anything we ever felt on earth. And contentment. We won't remember any hurts, fears, pain, or sadness. Only beautiful joy and everlasting peace. Jesus will be everything to us, and we will lack for nothing. God is love, and love never fails. Absent with the body, present with the Lord.

September 7, 2013

Blessed, blessed Lord. You have blessed me today, more than I can say. Ronald, my son, and I rode to PA to go to yard sales with Bart. What a blessing you have given me. Just to spend the day with my son, my Baby, and then on the way home, he told me that his new boss asked him questions before he hired him. The first question was, who did he look up to in his life, who was his role model, someone who meant the world to him and that he wanted to be just like. Ronald told him me! I almost cried, then the man said to him, "Have you ever told your mom that?" Ronald said he had not, but he told me today. Praise the Lord. I am more blessed every day.

October 7, 2013

Mrs. Ann Johnson is the wisest person I've ever met, I think. Mostly because she was led by the Holy Spirit and always loved me, in spite of me. Just like Jesus. She would also correct me and read me the Word always. She disciples me, and I'm not the same person I was when I met her because of her love for Jesus and how she showed it. She was originally Catholic but then got saved, and for some reason, Catholics make the best Christians!

It's a blessing in disguise. If we didn't have pain, we wouldn't know when something serious was wrong, and we could die sooner than if we felt the pain and got help.

Jesus gave me a wonderful dream last night. It looked like in my dream, it was the Puerto Rican day festivals because everyone there was either Spanish or Puerto Rican. This little boy about Caitlyn's age, maybe younger, was practicing a worldly song, and I was singing the counterpart. Finally, after three or four times, she got it right, and the room we were in filled up with people. They all were either Spanish or Puerto Rican. Everyone looked hard and worldly like bikers. Then we started singing our song. The young boy started just then when I sang the words that we had practiced and changed into words about Jesus. How much He loved us and how much He sacrificed so we could live a wonderful life in this world and the next. No matter how hard I tried, I could not sing the words we practiced, God's word came through my mouth instead, in the form of His word.

Everyone in the room had looks of shock and "how dare I" on their faces, especially the boy who practiced the song with me. I was very worried and scared, but I kept on singing about Jesus. When it was all over, everyone was silent. No one spoke a word. They look at each other and had tears running down their faces. At the end of my dream, all the families came together that had been separated. They were holding each other and crying with smiles on their face. Because of Jesus' name, a great restoration took place, thanks to the Holy Spirit, who changed my song to a heavenly song.

What a wonderful dream. At the name of Jesus, Philippians 2:10–11(NKJV),

> *that at the name of Jesus every knee should bow, of those in heaven, and of those on earth, and of those under the earth, and that every tongue should confess that Jesus Christ is Lord, to the glory of God the Father*

Jesus is the only one who can bring happiness through the obedience of His word. The most important gift we can give one another as human beings is unconditional love.

> *Your mercy O Lord, is in the heavens; Your faithfulness reaches to the clouds.*
> (Psalms 36:5 NKJV)

> *Oh, love of God, how rich and pure!*
> *How measureless and strong!*
> *It shall forevermore endure,*
> *The saints' and angels' song.*
>
> *Could we with ink the ocean fill,*
> *And were the skies of parchment made,*
> *Were every stalk on earth a quill,*
> *And every man a scribe by trade;*
> *To write the love of God above*
> *Would drain the ocean dry;*
> *Nor could the scroll contain the whole*
> *Though stretched from sky to sky.*
> ("The Love of God by Frederick M. Lehman, 1917" n.d.)

October 24, 2013

I feel my purpose in life has been to do two specific things;

1. To tell others about Christ's love for them.
2. To raise seven beautiful children in the fear and admonition of God.

Special Answers to Prayer:

Jesus is wonderful! Praise the name of my Lord and Savior!

I have been praying for thirteen years that my husband Billy would take my hand and pray with me. Not just grace for dinner, but a real prayer. Finally, after all these years, he was sitting on the edge of our bed, in the dark, and I said, "What are you doing?"

He said, "Sit here, and let's pray."

I was so overwhelmed I almost couldn't speak. I just took his hand, and he prayed. It was so beautiful, and it came from his heart—a long-awaited answer to my prayers.

The day before we went to Camp Okanicken with the Beacons' from Lighthouse Tabernacle, unbeknownst to me, Pastor Scramolie and Billy walked around the lake and talked. Jesus must have planned that day. Of course, He has our whole life planned, for better and for blessing. So, our job is to choose each day. Blessing or cursing, God's word says in Deuteronomy 30:19 (NKJV),

> I call heaven and earth as witnesses today against you, that I have set before you life and death, blessing and cursing; therefore choose life, that both you and your descendants may live.

November 7, 2013

Live in the present, it is a gift; that is why they call it the present. God's word says to "take no thought for the morrow" (Matthew 6:24 NKJV). All we have is this moment in time. Tomorrow is not promised.

> Only one life will soon be passed, only what's done for Christ will last.
> ("Quote by C.T. Studd" n.d.)

Orange, red, brown, gold, yellow, and green leaves are falling like huge colored snowflakes. It's funny or weird that when a tree dies, they are the most beautiful.

November 11, 2013

Dear Jesus, precious Lord,

*You are beautiful beyond description,
 too marvelous for words.
I stand, I stand in awe of you,
I stand, I stand in awe of you.
Holy God in whom all praise is due,
I stand in awe of you.*
("I Stand in Awe by Mark Altrogge, 1986" n.d.)

That is one of the most beautiful songs I like to sing.

"Rescued by a Fruit Cake"

*My fruitcake has a name,
I'll tell you who it is.
Not till my story ends,
One hint, it's not a "his".*

*It's a "her," and she was put on earth,
Because God loved me so.
She rescued me time and time again,
Always when I was low.*

*When she was a little girl,
I thought she needed lots of help.*

As it turned out, I never knew,
I needed help myself.

When she grew up, she moved far away.
I wish it were not so.
Cause once she saved my life,
When I was buried in the snow. (Millcreek Parkour van was buried)

Another time I needed her,
She came from far away.
She cooked and cleaned and drove my car
Till I was well
I wish she could have stayed.

She was someone else's daughter.
God gave her to me to love.
It's someone else's loss.
God pre-destined from above.

Her name is Debbie; she has rescued me time and time again.
She is kind and caring and loving
And a fruit cake
But she'll always be MY daughter and my friend.
She knows I love her very much,

So I can kid around with the time we have to spend.

So let me cut this short, my story has to end.
In the end, God' Word is true
We do reap what we sow.
I'm sure glad I sowed a little girl,
And reaped the woman that I love and know.
    (Naomi Jean Ortiz December 22, 2009)

—All my love to Deborah Lynne for being MY special little girl.

Heraclitus said, "There is nothing permanent except change" (n.d.) However, Jesus never fails; Jesus never changes. Thank God for this. He is the same, yesterday, today, and forever.

Jesus is love and tenderness personified.

He is tenderness and strength wrapped up in one, meekness and majesty, manhood and deity, velvet and steel. He embodies all the heroic qualities that humanity pines for.

CHAPTER 5

January 1, 2014

Praise God! Another new year and I am still here. I am old, but God is good. He has placed a melody in my heart and youthfulness upon my body and life. Mary Mako, my teacher in the Women's group for over twenty years, always used to say she didn't like people calling everything a miracle. She thought only things like a woman lifting a car off her child should be called a miracle. Well, I disagree. Every day of my life I see miracles that God has done for my family or me. He healed me of breast cancer and has prolonged Kay's life, which everyone thought she would die years ago. Ronald passed a kidney stone while in the ER, definitely God's touch. God has answered thousands of my prayers and my kid's prayers and even my grandchildren's prayers. Ronald's friend was touched when he found out Isaac, who is seven, prayed every night for him to be healed. God has healed my children, grandbabies, and me over and over and over again. Wonderful, merciful, compassionate God is our father and savior, Jesus Christ. Oh, that the whole world should come to know Him and the goodness of His love.

I never thought I would ever get my V.W. fixed! The estimate was $1100, and Billy is still on unemployment. But my merciful, wonderful, Father God had other plans. My brother Bart got a settlement from his lawyer for an accident he was in and was very generous with his money. He wrote me a check for $1100, which I must pay back, but I am able to take my time. I prayed that the bill would be less, so there would be no tax. When we went to pick up the car, they said, "You owe us nothing." God always answers my prayers, always.

Now getting back to miracles, even the little ones:

- When the sun shines.
- When the snow falls just enough and stops, so it doesn't bury the whole world.
- When you get hugged by your grandchildren.
- When right outside your window, there is a beautiful bird who is singing a melody to God.
- When the Holy Spirit speaks to my heart about sending an encouraging note to someone,

like our neighbor upstairs, Benjamin. Then he stopped to let us know how much he needed that note.
- When you see God's rainbow.
- When your husband buys you flowers and still loves you, in spite of your nagging.
- When God supplies necessities and monies on the "wings of a dove."
- When you receive an inheritance from someone who has passed.
- Everyday traveler's mercies. Once a car was heading straight for my car on a curve by the church. I closed my eyes and braced for the hit. Then I looked up and saw the car in its own lane. An angel intervened.
- My best friend and prayer partner Ginny underwent open-heart surgery at age eighty-two. You tell me that God wasn't there. God is real, and He answers prayer.

He is ever present and is more than worthy of our praises. He will never leave us or forsake us. His promises are true. This year 2013, I've had many heartaches, but the blessings of my Lord and Savior, Jesus Christ, far outweigh the bad. A very close friend of mine turned her back on me and a fifty-year-old friendship. I have no idea why. Jesus still loves me. My sister Joy, who I wanted to be close to all my life, turned her back on me, but Jesus never fails. I'm so thankful for Jesus. People hurt you and abuse you and leave you. But God is love and love never fails.

> *Oh give thanks to the Lord, for He is good! For his mercy endures forever. Oh, give thanks to the God of gods! For His mercy endures forever. Oh, give thanks to the Lord of lords! For His mercy endures forever.*
>
> (Psalm 136:1–3)

> *Behold, what manner of love the Father has bestowed on us, that we should be called children of God! Therefore, the world does not know us, because it did not know Him.*
>
> (1 John 3:1 NKJV)

January 2, 2014

Everything today is more difficult growing up than it was in my day when I grew up.

Song:

Jesus never fails.
Jesus never fails.

Heaven and earth may pass away.
But Jesus never fails.

("Jesus Never Fails
by Arthur A. Luther, 1927" n.d.)

January 24, 2014

Wondrous, beautiful, Holy God—I belong to you. I am yours, and you are mine. I appreciate you and all your attributes. You are constant, loving, and merciful. You are holy and forgiving, and always there. You are everything I've always needed and wanted in a friend, lover, confidant, Lord, Savior, husband, physician, brother, and God. No one can ever take Your place. I wouldn't want them to. Your beauty surrounds me constantly. Your faithfulness is like the morning sun. Your rainbow is surrounding me right now in my living room as I write. It is flowing over these pages, thank you, Jesus.

Right now, for us, my husband Billy is out of work, for the first time in thirteen years. His unemployment was canceled. We have nothing except my social security for old age. Jesus knows that and has been blessing us with the things we need. For instance, He granted us a rent subsidy just when we needed it. He is always on time. Never late. We also were able with God's favor, to get food stamps, and government help called, Soldier On, is going to help us with February's rent. Jesus never fails! Billy's brother, Danny, has been helping us with small side jobs too.

Housing has drastically changed. We live in a one-bedroom apartment, and it was $1070 for rent each month, which we could afford until Billy got laid off from G.S.A. It was almost impossible to pay rent after that until we were approved for rent subsidy in December. Now our rent is $876 for the same one-bedroom, but I only get $881 from Social security, too, so that leaves us with $5 for the whole month. God has been supplying our needs according to His riches in glory, but only when we needed it. Like the Israelites in the desert, we can't see it, but help is always there just in time—Manna when we are hungry and water when we thirst.

The overall quality of life has also changed drastically. Millions of people are hungry, out of work, or have lost their homes. We are blessed... we belong to God, and His word says, He will never see His kids begging bread... (Psalms 37:25)). The world today is backward and upside down. Just like God's Word says again, in the end times good will be evil, and evil will be good. (2 Timothy 3:13). That is exactly how society is today. Homosexuality is rampant and idolized by everyone. It is on almost every TV show, and no one cares. You can see Satan in all the movies that are produced, even the children's ones. God help us...

National and world politics have changed drastically today compared to when I was growing up. President Obama, our first black president, seems like he is trying to help everyone, but the Democrats and the Republicans are fighting so much in congress, and whatever else they vote on, no one can agree or get along with anyone else. They need to vote on our unemployment extension, but no one cares. They don't even have a date for it to be on the agenda. Meanwhile, everyone in politics is deliberately lying to us and saying the country is doing well and getting better. But if you look around and have half of a brain, you can see a depression- not a recession.

There have not been many significant medical advances or cures in my lifetime. Cancer is killing everyone because of all the artificial garbage they put in our food. Our water is poisoned, and the air we breathe is toxic. Medicine is going backward instead of forwards. If anyone did ever find a cure, it would be millions of dollars, and only the rich would benefit. The internet, meanwhile, is like a direct umbilical cord to Satan himself—from his loins into all our homes. That and the television, nothing on it is noteworthy.

Transportation hasn't changed too much, except for cars that brake and park themselves, which I think is extremely dangerous. There is a smart car too, which is a glorified tuna fish can. It looks like two people in a seat, and the car was spray-painted on them after they sat down! Haha, ha! We still have planes and trains, which are also so expensive that no one but the rich can afford to ride them.

Changes in communication from then to now is a laugh and a half. Everyone, even children, has cell phones. Everywhere you go, their phones are attached to their ears, and they are texting, even while driving. Many innocent people are being killed because people can't drive and text at the same time.

Lord, I sometimes forget that my efforts cannot earn Your love or grace or forgiveness. You have lavished grace on me as a gift, and not a wage. Thank you. In the realm of grace, the word 'deserve' does not apply.

"Isn't He Beautiful?"

February 22, 2014

Last night God made a beautiful rainbow that stretched across the endless sky. A storm had just ended, then came the beauty—kind of like our lives. We go "through" many storms. But God is so good that at the end of everyone, there is a beautiful rainbow. I am sixty-six years old and have never been forsaken or forgotten by my God. God is love, and love never fails.

Read 1 Corinthians 13—the whole chapter... it is very good.

Right now, in my life, we have been living by faith alone. Hebrews 11:1–10 (KJV), "without faith it is impossible to please Him." Since December 28th of last year, 2013, we have been totally living by faith in our Lord and Savior, Jesus Christ, and His word. Billy was severed from his job last May. Then in December, the US Congress took away everyone's unemployment extension benefits. So, we have nothing except my Social Security for old age, and our faith in God. Thank God for my childhood. My mom and dad took us to Sunday School and church, as well as Bible School in the summer. The Holy Spirit instilled tons of God's word in my heart. He brings it to the surface like a bubbling spring. When I am in need of uplifting, it just comes up in me. Also, God has been performing many, many miracles in our lives since there is nothing else to help us but Him. We had no rent money in February or March. God sent us a place called Soldier On, who paid for February's rent, then we got our income tax done and that paid March's rent. Also, Pastor Scramolie called us with a $300 gift that someone in our church gave to us anonymously. May God bless those people who helped.

Also, in December of 2013, we received help with our rent amounts and heating assistance, food stamps, and even help with our phone. Wonderful, wonderful Lord. Every day is a new surprise, like Christmas.

The influence of mass media in our society and the world has had help from our enemy. Since the enemy of our souls has come into all of our homes through the TV, internet, and radio. God showed me an umbilical cord from Satan, the deceiver, from his bowels into the cable that runs through over homes. Unless you are rooted or grounded in God's Word, the internet and TV will influence your life to destruction. Remember, God's Word tells us the enemy of our souls is out to "steal, kill, and destroy" (John 10:10 KJV). His only purpose is to blind us to God's Word and love. Keep steadfast, immovable in Christ.

April 6, 2014

Yesterday, we waited for the result of Caitlyn's MRI. Because of her headaches, they are trying to find a reason. Praise God. Jesus never fails. The results were excellent. The lesions they found in her brain on the first MRI were almost all gone, and the few that were left had stayed the same. No one but Jesus knows why she is having headaches. Now the doctors are going to check her for lime disease. Dr. Dunn, the doctor who collects penguins, said, "Personally, I think she has nothing wrong with her except she doesn't eat or drink right." She goes nowhere and gets no exercise, and the main reason for her headaches is that her mother and father scream all the time at each other and don't know how to talk normally to anyone, including her and me. If her life changed, her headaches would disappear. I can only pray that God will help her.

April 6, 2014

I was single and wished I stayed that way. Except for the blessings of my beautiful children and grandchildren. Then I was divorced from a loveless marriage where he raped me. Then I was widowed by Frank, whom I loved with all my heart. He passed into heaven. Then I married Ronald Sr., whom I also loved, but he left me for someone younger. Then he divorced me. I stayed alone for over ten years and ran my business. Then I met Mr. Ortiz and married again because I was lonely.

I don't remember what I wrote about our living conditions now. But this is definitely one of the hardest times in my life. There is $0 income from work, but God has been bringing in gifts and money on the wings of a dove, a retired man in my church gave us a check for $2,000. I was so overjoyed and happy; I couldn't stop crying and thanking God. We also got food stamps and heating assistance, which helps. I found out that Francis E. Jr., my deceased husband, did have an insurance policy, and we are getting $247, not much, but compared to nothing, it is a real blessing.

I am living my life for Jesus Christ, my children and my grandchildren, my husband, and myself, in that order. I've been praying for Ronald and Bethany and the kids to stay here in New Jersey. Bethany's mom wants to buy her a house in Arkansas. I can't stand the thought of losing them. Jesus knows, and I want God's will for all their lives. My heart will break if they leave. Please, Lord Jesus, keep them near me. I will write again about the miracles I know God is going to do for them and me.

My health is very good now. God healed me of the pain I was having in my groin and of breast cancer. I didn't even realize the pain was gone. I couldn't sit, stand, or walk; it was always there when I did those things. Then one day, I had some trouble with my left eye again. The one I went blind in when I was twenty-two. I forgot all about the pain, and one day realized it was gone. Praise the Lord! For He is good, all the time. His mercy endures forever, through all generations (Psalm 100:5).

All the while I am writing, my rainbow maker, which is a crystal with a solar panel, is circling the entire room. It's so beautiful. It reminds me of God's love, faithfulness, and His many promises.

My pet peeves are being late and people who are late. Drivers who text and don't know how to drive courteously. Baggie ties, baggies that do not have a zipper and never close properly. Billy leaves drawers and doors open. He makes sandwiches on top of the open drawers, so I have to scoop out all the crumbs—every time. He has not worked now for almost one year since May 2013.

April 15, 2014, Tuesday

Jesus precious Jesus! Sunday, I was in Pastor Scramolie's class, and Jesus healed me of eye pain. For two days, Saturday and Sunday, I had pain in my left eye. Everyone in Sunday School gathered in a circle and prayed for everyone. I felt the Holy Spirit so strong that I cried and cried. When the prayer was over, my left eye was healed. Praise the Lord, for He is good all the time.

Also, last week, Billy started work, after almost one year of being unemployed. Praise God. He won't get his first check till the 18th of April, but at least he is working. He is doing maintenance work for Burlington County Community College in Pemberton.

Talking about my personal concerns is a touchy subject. I'm sure in the pages to come, there will be a wonderful personal testimony of how God answered my prayers. But for now, I am very concerned about Caitlyn, my granddaughter leaving home with her new friend Savannah. She flew in all the way from California to stay with Caitlyn. A total stranger to us. God answers prayers.

Also, I'm concerned about Ronald Jr. and Bethany and Isaac, the twins, and Jayden moving to Arkansas. Linda and David Scott, Bethany's mom and dad after years and years of not seeing her or the kids, have taken the money they supposedly saved and bought themselves and Ronald and Bethany a house in Mountain Home, Arkansas on Fish and Fiddle Road, not kidding, that is the name. My heart is broken, and I am devastated but still believing that my God will answer my prayers and keep them here. I do want God's perfect will for their lives, and I do know they are anointed to teach and preach, and Bethany has a beautiful voice, but I am selfish, I guess, I love them so much. Especially

Isaac. Billy and I raised him the whole first year of his life. So, he is closest to us. And Ronald Jr. is my baby, my youngest. I don't want to lose any of them. My prayer is they will stay here, and God will do a miracle for them.

Nothing in what is going on in the world concerns me because God is still on the throne, and He is in control of everything.

May 1, 2014

Right now, I'm praying that my son Ronald and his family will not move to Arkansas—Unless it is God's perfect will. When I think about what's happening, my heart sinks into depression. I have to fight to be happy again.

Also, Pastor McKenna is letting go of Pastor Scramolie and Jeanie. He is my Sunday School teacher and the leader of our Beacons group for those over fifty. We are all devastated and hurt, and no one will tell us why.

When things like this happen, and life feels like the bottom is dropping out, I need to pray and read my Bible and sing God's joyful songs. I also want to make a list of all the times God' saved me and from what He saved me from. Jesus never fails. Heaven and earth may pass away, but Jesus never fails (Matthew 24:35.

1. God saved me from me when I was twelve, and again when I was thirty-two.
2. God saved me from drowning three times. Once in a cement pool with my friends from my youth group. Dianna Cross pulled me out. Second time in Chester Creek. I went through a tire tube with my head stuck underwater. My mom pulled me out. The third time in the Sun Oil pool, my mom pulled me out again.
3. God saved me through three live births, and three miscarriages and three abortions. I was forgiven and set free.
4. God saved me through fourteen major surgeries. One was cancer, and three were hernias.
5. God saved me from the jungle in Haiti and brought me home safe.
6. He saved me from a parasite that seemed to be eating me alive.
7. Seven is God's number of completions. He saved me from the world to tell about His love for the lost and dying.

I have a great peace of mind because God has given me that peace of mind through all life's trials and disappointments and all life's valleys. Whenever it was the darkest, God's light always shone through. His word is true, and His love is constant, and His mercy endures through all generations (Psalms 100:5). He has never stopped loving me, even when I've failed Him. He is a wonderful and loving Father, Lord, and Savior, Healer, Friend, Confidant, Shield, and a Brother like no other. He is always faithful to the end.

June 9, 2014

I think there is an intellectual me; I used to contemplate very long and deep about my God when I was in the Baptist church—About there had to be more than what they were teaching us. Just to be saved and be baptized, and that was all there was. I knew Jesus and also knew that there was much more to Him than this religion was preaching. I found out there was lots more when I started Lighthouse Tabernacle Church. I changed from Baptist to Pentecostal, and then realized the fullness of my God.

June 9, 2014—2:30 a.m.

My smile is one of my best qualities, which is the joy of the Lord, really. I am Sixty-seven years old today by the grace and mercy of Jesus. I am alive and well and very, very blessed because God loves me.

This has been one of the most heart wrenching and difficult times in my life.

My son, Ronald and his wife Bethany, Isaac, the twins, and Jayden moved to Arkansas. They are in Virginia as we speak, which is not quite halfway to their new home. My heart is grieved, but I know I will see them again. God has done several miracles for them on this trip. They broke down the first night in Maryland. In a place with no houses or stores. AAA would not help them because they were towing their auto with their van. So, they were stranded, when all of a sudden, this man, I'm sure God sent him, came to where they were with a tow truck and stopped to help them. He owned his own shop. I think God sent an angel. They stayed at Era's house for three or four days, which is another sweet coincidence that God provided. Praise His name. Then they checked into a hotel in Virginia because their van, the KIA, was not going to be completed till Tuesday. Almost a week away. God also took care of the hotel too. Ronald found a hotel for $500 for two rooms but wasn't ready. He walked across the street to Motel 6 and found one large room for everyone for $340 all the way to Tuesday. Praise the Lord! Isn't He wonderful!

A song by Laura Story, I just thought of, and I'm sure it was by the Holy Spirit is called *Blessings* says,

> *What if your blessings came though rain drops,*
> *what if your healing come through tears?*
> *What if a thousand sleepless night are what it takes to know He's near.*
> *What if the trials of this life are His blessings in disguise?*
>
> ("Laura Story - Blessings, 2011" n.d.)

I handle stress by giving it over and over again to Christ. That is very, very hard to do. Besides getting used to my kids living thousands of miles away, I also lost my church too. I would need a whole separate book to write about what the devil is causing there. We must be very close to Jesus' return because all hell is breaking loose, and many people are turning to Jesus also. People are lovers of self, like the Bible says, even Pastors. This all started with Pastor McKenna kicking Pastor Scramolie and his wife Jeanie out of our church—for NO good reason.

The basic philosophy I live by is Jesus was crucified, is living, and is coming again. There can be no other.

It's 3:30 a.m., I am falling asleep. I must write again later. Love You, Lord, Jesus, and thank you for helping Ronald and his family. Thank you for my birthday. Every day I see Your hand upon my life and my kids' and grandkids' lives. New miracles every day, as life goes by so fast, it's hard to write them all down.

June 19, 2014

My greatest contribution to life has been for me to tell others about Jesus—as well as helping the needy and homeless, and ministering in church in music and Stephens Ministry, and raising my beautiful children in the fear of God. Loving and helping raise my grandchildren. Writing this book that may someday, if Jesus tarries, lead someone to Jesus.

It's almost midnight, and I can't sleep. I'm not sure why, I think, because I'm depressed about Ronald and his family moving so far away and also losing my church, along with the Beacons. Plus, it was the hottest day of the year so far.

I am glad Jesus loves me and will never leave. If it weren't for Him, I wouldn't want to be here for one second. I'm sure that He is taking me to a new place in Him. were someday, He will be able to help someone with the life experiences He has taken me through and safely brought me out of, to the other side.

I don't want to be remembered for anything else than knowing through my friendship, fellowship or mothering, someone or several people have gotten to know Jesus by the light in my life that He has given to me. Or that they have gotten closer to Him by remembering my life or reading this book. There will never be any good thing in Naomi (me) except His Holy Spirit. Only by His Spirit moving through me to others is how I hope to be remembered.

God is taking me through lots of changes. Some are deep, dark valleys, some are mountain tops, beautiful with rainbow experiences. He is always teaching me something new. I only hope and pray I remain pliable and teachable in my master's hands.

"Rebellion, it is as the sin of witchcraft" (1 Samuel 1:15 KJV). I pray I never fall away or rebel against my Lord and Savior. He knows me better than anyone. Sometimes I run out ahead of Him, then I fall. But I learn a very good lesson. "...Be still and know that I am God..." (Psalm 46:10 KJV). I need all the help I can get to be still and allow Him to move. I pray every day for His strength to be made perfect in my weakness. When I am weakest, He is strong (2 Corinthians 12:10).

July 23, 2014—1:10 a.m.

> *Wonderful Jesus!*
> *I'm so happy and here's the reason why.*
> *Jesus took my burdens all away.*
> *Now I'm singing as the days go by.*

Jesus took my burdens all away.
Once my heart was heavy with a load of sin.
Jesus took the load and gave me peace within.
Now I'm singing as the days go by,
Jesus took my burdens all away.

("I'm So Happy
by Stanton W. Gavitt, 1936" n.d.)

Praise His name forever. He is more than worthy to be praised!

- My favorite book is my King James Bible. Why? Because it was my Father's last will and testament to me. All the secrets of the Universe lie in His written word. And so does all His power.
- My favorite song is This is Only the World by Mandisa. This song reminds me that this is not my home. I'm only passing through. Heaven is my ultimate destination.
- My favorite movie is Liar, Liar and Oh, God because I laughed so hard, I almost couldn't breathe.
- My favorite color is orange because it's a happy, bright color that matches all that God has done for me.
- My favorite food is eggs, bacon, and cheese on a croissant. Why? Because it just is.

- My favorite gift is the Holy Spirit in my life and Jesus' sacrifice for me. Why? It's obvious by now, God saved me from eternal hell.
- My favorite flower is the orange Tiger Lilly.
- My favorite holiday is Mother's Day. It would be Christmas if our world didn't commercialize it so much. If we all just celebrated Jesus' birthday, then that day would be the best.
- My favorite actresses are Marilyn Monroe and Jennifer Aniston.
- My favorite joke is this one. Little Boy who learned in Sunday School that we all came from dust and return to dust. When he arrived home from church and went up to his room, he came running down a few minutes later and hollered to his mother, "There is someone under my bed!" …and "he is either coming or going."
- My favorite singer is Mandisa, a Christian in today's music. The Beatles for secular must because I really liked them when I was young.
- My favorite type of music is Christian Music only.
- My favorite sports team is the Eagles. I don't even know why. I don't like sports on TV, or in person.

- My favorite television show is Third Rock from The Sun. it was people who came from another planet, and everything they saw and did was funny and strange. Dick and Sally were the lead characters.
- My favorite perfume is Sunflower.
- My favorite author is God and all the different people that God inspired to write the Holy Bible.
- My favorite season is Fall. The sides of a whole mountain are the colors of purple, blue, green, orange, red, yellow, and brown—almost like the colors of a rainbow.
- My favorite recipe is Avgolemono (Chicken Lemon Soup). It has two cans of chicken broth, 1 whole lemon, 1/3 cup of rice, and three eggs— Cook the chicken broth as directed until it boils. Add rice until it is fully cooked, remove from heat, add the juice of one lemon and three beaten eggs. So the eggs don't cook, add some of the hot soup to the eggs while beating.
- My favorite leisure activity is riding bicycles down at the beach in Ocean City or Virginia Beach.
- My favorite political leader was Abraham Lincoln. Lincoln freed the slaves and was a Godly

man who had a very hard life, but he overcame it.
- My hero is, of course, Jesus. No question why!
- I have two favorite artists, my mother and Van Gogh.
- My favorite pick me up is Boost or drink a toast, flat coke syrup.
- My favorite quotes are:
    - God is love, and love never fails(1 Corinthians 13:8)
    - "I can do all things through Christ who strengthens me" (Philippians 4:13 NKJV).
    - "Greater is He that is in me, than he that is in the world" (1John 4:4 KJV).
    - "I will never leave you nor forsake you" (Hebrews 13:5 NKJV).
    - "I am with you always, even unto the end of the world" (Matthew 28:20). Jesus said both of those last two statements.
- My favorite snack food is cucumbers and radishes.
- My favorite vacation spot is Ocean City or Virginia Beach.

June 20, 2014

One of our family traditions is going to the beach every summer and the mountains every winter. When Mom and Dad were alive, we would go to Ocean City every summer. The city there was cleaner and quieter. It's a dry town, meaning there is no alcohol allowed there. Then Dad's relatives all lived in Scranton and Moosic, the Poconos Mountains. So, every winter we would go to visit them. I had a favorite cousin named June. She became my best friend. I saw her only once or twice a year, but we wrote all year long. When we got together, we'd go to Rocky Glenn Park and go Roller Skating. We'd always have fun. She was a few years older than me.

All my family on Mom and Dad's side were all born-again Christians from generations back. We lived under God's special blessings because of our bloodline. Dad's side was Pentecostal, and Mom's side was Baptist. They all loved the Lord and worshiped Jesus Christ. So, all my life, I was blessed no matter what came my way. We had lots of family get-togethers. But both sides were so large, it was hard to fit them all in one place. Mom was the oldest of seven with spouses and lots of kids. Dad was the oldest of twenty-one with spouses and kids. With his mom and dad and hers, and just the siblings and spouses, it was sixty people, not counting the children.

The most important thing I would want family and friends to remember about me is Jesus never failed me, not even once. Even when I failed Him, He was always there—nothing much to know about me. I was always very happy and full of joy because of Jesus. Sometimes I was down or hurt, but it never lasted too long. I love to pray but had to force myself to read, even the Bible. I started with the devotional *Our Daily Bread*, which is a daily devotional. I enjoy simple food and family and simple friends. I enjoy most of all rainbows, riding bikes, sunsets, breakfast, surprises, family, especially my grandchildren, eating out, driving my V.W. Bug, telling others about Jesus.

The misconception I want to straighten out is that I didn't marry four times because I wanted to. I wanted to be married to one husband for life. My life became very complicated. My first husband raped me. I was sixteen, and he was twenty-two, and my parents made us get married—Big mistake. They should have had him arrested. I fell in love, very deep love with Francis E. Vail Jr. when I was twenty, and he was thirty. I left Arthur to be with Frank. He was wonderful. He loved me very much but died when he was forty-two, of malignant melanoma—leaving me with his four kids and my own son James. I met Ronald Sr. when he was nineteen, and I was 32. We were married and had Ronald Jr. Ronald Sr. left us in 1991.

There is an issue I feel very strongly about but have mostly kept to myself, which is I don't like; actually, I hate racism. I don't like the way white people treat black people or other races and vice versa. I see no differences in any people; under the skin, we are all the same.

Secondly, President Obama only got elected because he was black. People who had never voted, came to the polls just to vote for him. They didn't care what he even stood for, only that he was their same skin color.

Thirdly, people of all races who have the most influence are the people who have all the money. Such a shame...

My mother's brothers were all crazy. My uncle James was always patting my butt. My uncle Joey was always teasing me until I cried. Mostly he would bad mouth my mom. My uncle Phillip we can't even find, but he was a bank robber. When he got out of prison, he became a missionary but disappeared just before Granny died.

On my dad's side, I had an Uncle Billy, who was gay, but he was very nice to me. He always brought me crystals from the mines in the mountains. They called them Pennsylvania Deborahs. I collected different rocks and gems.

September 3, 2014

We are leaving for Arkansas on the 13th of this month. Even though I hate to fly, I need to be with my son Ronald and his kids—especially Isaac. I miss them all very badly. We will be staying for two weeks and coming home on the 27th. God is so good. I can't wait to go. I am praying for extra money to spend, so I can pay my bills and still go. I am also praying for Bethany's mom, Linda, who has been harassing them and making their life miserable. We all knew that this would happen as soon as she bought them that house. Now she is holding the house over their heads to get them to do everything she wants. It's a shame. She needs a lot of prayers.

September 9, 2014

I don't need any wishes because my God has supplied all my needs, "according to His riches in glory," for all my life (Philippians 4:19 KJV).

October 3, 2014

Praise the Lord, for He is good. He always, always answers prayer and is there when I need Him. I thank you, Lord, with all my heart and soul, for you are more than worthy to be praised.

We returned safe, of course, from Arkansas on September 27. Once on a tiny express jet, and then on a huge Boeing 707. Both were choppy flights and with wonderful pilots. We took off from Philadelphia International in the rain but landed in North Carolina with beautiful sunshine. All the way there, I was talking to God and He to me. Amazing how faithful our God is.

In North Carolina, the midway flight, He showed me a beautiful rainbow in the clouds, on a sunny day, with no rain. That was His way of telling me that He was there with me, and all His promises to me were still yea and amen. Then He spoke to my heart when I asked Him for a safe journey and to hold up our plane. He said, "Haven't I always been with you? All your life, I was there. Every breath you have taken in sixty-seven years have come from me. When you went into a cold operating room with no one else except a surgeon, and his nurse, I was there. Every time you needed no morphine drip after surgeries because you had no pain, I was there. When you were a child and almost drowned, I pulled you from the water three times. When you had your children, I was there, especially your daughter Candy."

The umbilical cord was around her neck more than once. She was a miracle baby. But so was Ronald. I had a tubal ligation before Ronald, and then You gave me him. You were there that night, a stranger walked into my mom and Dad's house and started up the steps to my room after midnight. Then He turned around and left. You never left me or my kids or my grandkids, and I'm confident You never, never will.

One day we were there in Arkansas, and I got sick with irritable bowel syndrome (I.B.S.). I went to the Mountain Home hospital, and they gave me Flagyl. It worked wonderfully with my diet—No dairy and no fried foods. While I was picking up my medications in Walmart, a female store employee asked me if she could help me. I said, "Yes," and told her my dilemma. She put her hand on my back and said, "God bless you," while she silently prayed for me. Thank you, Jesus, for sending an angel.

I also remember the angel you sent me in the hospital here in New Jersey, at 3:00 a.m. when I awoke and was afraid. A nurse, or angel, really, came into my room and held my hand and sang to me the song, *What a Friend We Have in Jesus*. You sent her, my beautiful Lord and Savior. I will never forget what You did. Thank you, it seems so small to say when all You've done is so great and amazing.

Today's Bible Reading—Psalm 136:1–9, 23–26 (NKJV):

Oh, give thanks to the Lord, for He is good!
For His mercy endures forever.
Oh, give thanks to the God of gods!
For His mercy endures forever.
Oh, give thanks to the Lord of lords!
For His mercy endures forever:
To Him who alone does great wonders,
For His mercy endures forever;
To Him who by wisdom made the heavens,
For His mercy endures forever;
To Him who laid out the earth above waters,
For His mercy endures forever;
To Him who made great lights,
For His mercy endures forever—
The sun to rule by day,
For His mercy endures forever;
The moon and stars to rule by night,
For His mercy endures forever...
Who remembered us in our lowly state,
For His mercy endures forever, and rescued us from
  our enemies,
For His mercy endures forever;
Who gives food to all flesh,
For His mercy endures forever.

> *Oh, give thanks to the God of heaven!*
> *For His mercy endures forever.*

November 5, 2014

Wonderful blessings have been falling down like rain. Billy started his new job on the last day of October. It's so nice to have things back to normal. He also loves his job.

Uncle Alvin died but is in peace in heaven. We had a wonderful Kounnas reunion on November 1st in PA. It was so nice to see everyone that I haven't seen for years: aunts and uncles and so many cousins, like Timmy and even Joy. The food was great, but the fellowship was greater. Also, Holly got free tickets to the Media Theater. They were showing *The Addams Family*, a live play. It was a real nice night out with dinner also. I don't care much for musicals, but it was certainly different.

God did something very special, like He always does, especially for me. He answered my prayers once again and kept Caitlyn home from California. Everyone in my new church was praying. This is another blessing, our new church. It's called Full Gospel Fellowship, where Pastor Bob and Dana are our leaders. The sweetest people you'd ever want to know.

I bumped into a man and his wife in the Dollar Tree, who asked me if Caitlyn ever came back from California. I told them that, "God stopped her from even going. Praise the Lord." They said, "Wonderful; we were praying for her." God is so awesome. People I only knew casually from McDavid's were praying, and I never knew it. But God knew it, isn't He wonderful?

Yesterday I got a buy-one-get-one-free Burger King croissant for breakfast—bacon, egg, and cheese. So, I couldn't figure out what to do with the other one. I looked for a homeless person and found one a minute later. She was in a wheelchair, next to the new C.V.S. Pharmacy. I got out of my car and asked her if she wanted the extra croissant, and she said yes, and thank you. Then as I was getting back in my car, she said, "Wait a moment. Do you like Salmon?" I said, "Yes." She said, come and get this and gave me a large can of Bumble Bee Salmon. I put it in my car and said thank you, then she said, "Do you like canned ham?" I said, "Yes." Then she gave me one and also potato chips and Martinelli's sparkling cider. I couldn't believe how God blessed me again. I gave away food that cost $1.50 and got back about $25.00 worth of food. God is so good, all the time.

The best part of all my recent blessings from my precious Heavenly Father is what happened to me last Sunday. My new sister Vernita Bell who cooks our food in church all the time is also a prayer warrior. She hugged me and prayed for my healing, which I received, then she proceeded to tell me that God has been saving me for such a time as this. He has been hiding me from the enemy. He is getting ready to move me out into ministry in these end times. My Spirit got a witness to this because it had been my prayer for years. Finally! I can't wait. My Spirit leaped for joy.

We are waiting for a good report from our Pastor Bob. He has malignant Myeloma cancer and is in the hospital. We are all praying for God to heal his body. We love him and need him back. Even on Tuesday, our cancer group is not the same without him. Just a bunch of gossipy old ladies. He made us better, and it was worth going to be there with him. I really miss him. He is like a very special brother to me. I pray, dear Lord for a mighty miracle healing and a return to us. We just go to know him and love him, and now he is gone. Please, Lord, God, we want him back with us. I remember when he called Doris's husband a "stud muffin." She got so embarrassed. But he was just one of us being funny. He joked with all of us but was really afraid of this cancer. I don't blame him, but our God is mightier than any disease or sickness, an enemy or Goliath, or devil in hell. He commands the ocean tides, the moon and sun, and stars. He speaks, and the winds obey. He can certainly take cancer away from our sweet Pastor Bob. I believe in Jesus' name, and I cover and hide him in the precious blood of Jesus Christ—in the rock of ages, I hide him. Greater is he that is in me, than he that is in the world (1 John 4:4). Amen.

November 18, 2014

Today is Tuesday. My youngest daughter, Candy, was born forty-one years ago today. She was a miracle baby. After my first child, James, was born in 1965, the doctor told me I could not carry another child full-term. I had three spontaneous miscarriages. Then I was pregnant with Candy. I had to take hormones to help keep her. I carried her for nine months; then, when I went to deliver, the cord was around her neck more than once. My doctor couldn't get her to come down the birth canal. He was ready to give up and said he almost cried when finally, she was born. She was a miracle.

Yesterday I almost lost my youngest son Ronald., but thanks be to our marvelous Savior, Jesus Christ, he is alive and well today. Ronald was on his way home from work when a large spider came from inside the visor of his van. Ronald took his eyes off the road to kill the spider. When he did, all the traffic in front of him stopped to look at a police car. By the time he looked back ahead, it was too late to stop. His van was totaled. By the Grace of our wonderful, all-merciful God, he was saved and is ok. Thank you, thank you, thank you, Jesus. It seems so little to say to such a loving Savior, not only for all the times He has saved my children, grandchildren, and me but for His unspeakable gift at Calvary. I owe Him my life.

Martin Luther, not Martin Luther King, wrote a beautiful song. A mighty fortress is our God.

CHAPTER 6

February 12, 2015

God is on the throne. He is still good, all the time.

Last night I went to Wednesday p.m. service at Full Gospel Fellowship. Pastor Bob Ingram preached. I love that man. He is very special to God and to me. But he preached something that I know is wrong. But I'm going to keep it between God and me for now. Pastor Bob said, "God doesn't want us to be happy." I'm sorry, but he is dead wrong! God is our heavenly Father, and just as our earthly father wants us to be happy, so does God. Only 10,000 times more. He just has a desire in His heart that far exceeds our happiness, and that is desiring to spend eternity with us. So, in other words, if what makes us happy will send us to hell for eternity. He doesn't allow it. Actually, we reap what we sow. Like in the book of Job in the Bible, which we read last night, we have certain things in our life that draw us to Father God. Like cancer and diabetes, they don't make us happy, but the greater importance is eternal life with our Creator, Jesus Christ, not happiness. So, our Heavenly Father allows unhappy, not so nice things to happen in our lives to draw us to Him. Like the scripture says, "it is better that we live with one eye, or if one arm offends us... than to spend eternity in hell, separated from Father God. I hope that's what Pastor Bob meant (Matthew 18:9). Because I know my Heavenly Father well, and He does want us to be happy, not to the point that our happiness is causing us to be separated from Him, our God.

July 12, 2019

Final Entry to Close My Book

Speaking of unhappiness. I'm seventy-two now and lost my rights to see my grandchildren at the hands of my youngest son, whom I adore. I haven't seen him or his children in months. My heart is broken.

Also, I have contracted breast cancer for the third time, after God healed me of it twice before. I am refusing surgery or chemo because I believe God has healed me again, this time without my Doctors. My husband

and children all want me to have surgery because this is how they believe I will be healed. God can do anything. He saved me from eternal hell and myself. He died and suffered great agony so that I could be healed. Praise His Name, for He is good all the time. I gave God permission over my life and my body to do anything He has for His Glory or to keep me in His Will. I am therefore expecting great things. I will soon be able to see my son and his children, and I will soon be healed. Body, soul, and Spirit. If it even means that my healing is to go to Heaven. That is the ultimate healing. I am at peace with whatever God wants for me.

Please rejoice with me. If I end up staying here and being healed or seeing Jesus in Heaven, either way, I want God's Will.

July 20, 2019

My last thoughts for this book are for you who are reading. If you have never asked Jesus to be your Lord and Savior, do it today. Don't delay. Tomorrow may never come. It's very simple. You don't need a church or a pastor or a priest to pray to God. Just bow your head in a quiet place, closet, bathroom, or literally any place and pray this prayer.

Dear Lord Jesus,

Please hear my prayer. I want to ask you to be my Lord and Savior. I believe you died on Calvary for me, so my sins could be forgiven. Please forgive me of all my sins. I believe You are God, and I ask You to come into my heart and life and be my Lord. Change me to be like You, for I know You are Holy.

In Jesus Name,
Amen!

Now you belong to God and are His child for eternity. He loved you already and knew you before time began. You will never die an eternal death, only your body. Your spirit man will live forever with God in Heaven. All your family and friends will be waiting at the gate to welcome you to Heaven. It will be a great reunion

Now do your best, with Jesus' help, to live for God. Read your Bible every day and get in a good Bible-believing church to fellowship with other believers. It will make your life here on earth much easier and happier.

Remember, " ...the joy of the Lord is your strength" (Nehemiah 8:10 NKJV). Always and forever.

I will meet you someday soon at the pearly gates.

It is well with my soul. It is well; it is well with my soul.

Rain vs Rain

> While water from the heavens makes the flower petals bounce.
> "Send the rain" we pray to Jesus, and cannot drink an ounce.
> My soul cries out for mercy and answers to my prayers.
> My Father knows the outcome, and I know He truly cares.
> The heart pain of this burden should not be felt by me.
> Before my birth, my Jesus took every woe by hanging on a tree.
> When Father watched as time began, He knew this too would come.
> He had a plan, a perfect plan; He sacrificed His son.
> When deep sadness dries up all hope, and burdens drag your soul apart.
> Know this, my friend for sure, that Jesus never took you from His Heart.

He is there and cares and loves you more than you could ever see.
With love you can't imagine, He died for you and me.

(Naomi Jean Ortiz, May 2, 2019)

References

"Change My Heart Oh Lord by Eddie Espinos, 1982." n.d. Divine Hymns.Com. Accessed February 25, 2020. http://www.divinehymns.com/lyrics/change-my-heart-oh-lord-song-lyrics/.

"Great Is Thy Faithfulness by Thomas O. Chisholm, 1923." n.d. Hymnary.Org. Accessed February 26, 2020. https://hymnary.org/text/great_is_thy_faithfulness_o_god_my_fathe.

"Hymn: Praise God, from Whom All Blessings Flow by Thomas Ken, 1673." 2020. Hymnal.Net. 2020. https://www.hymnal.net/en/hymn/h/8.

"I'm So Happy by Stanton W. Gavitt, 1936." n.d. Accessed February 26, 2020. http://hymnal.calvarybcsv.org/273.html.

"I Stand in Awe by Mark Altrogge, 1986." n.d. Sovereign Grace Music. Accessed February 26, 2020. https://sovereigngracemusic.org/music/songs/i-stand-in-awe/.

"It Took a Miracle." n.d. Jesus Is Savior.Com. Accessed February 25, 2020. https://www.jesus-is-savior.com/sounds/Hymns/it_took_a_miracle.htm.

"Jesus Never Fails by Arthur A. Luther, 1927." n.d. Hymnary.Org. Accessed February 26, 2020. https://hymnary.org/text/earthly_friends_may_prove_untrue.

"Laura Story - Blessings, 2011." n.d. Azlyrics.Com. Accessed February 26, 2020. https://www.azlyrics.com/lyrics/laurastory/blessings.html.

"Lift Me Up Lyrics." 2020. Lyrics.Com. 2020. https://www.lyrics.com/lyric/21027833/The+Afters/Lift+Me+Up.

"My Hope Is Built on Nothing Less by Edward Mote, 1834." n.d. Hymnary.Org. Accessed February 25, 2020. https://hymnary.org/text/my_hope_is_built_on_nothing_less.

"Nursery Rhyme, Thomas Fleet, 1737." 2020. New Haven Register. 2020. https://www.nhregister.com/news/article/GODSQUAD-Now-I-lay-me-down-to-sleep-prayer-has-11540927.php.

"Quote by C.T. Studd." n.d. Web Truth.Org. Accessed February 21, 2020. https://www.webtruth.org/great-quotes/quotes-c-t-studd/.

"Quote by Heraclitus." n.d. Brainy Quote. Accessed February 26, 2020. https://www.brainyquote.com/quotes/heraclitus_165537.

"Quote by Maya Angelou." n.d. Brainy Quote. Accessed February 26, 2020. https://www.brainyquote.com/quotes/maya_angelou_148650.

"Quote by Quentin Tarantino." 2020. Quotefancy. 2020. https://quotefancy.com/quote/892507/Quentin-Tarantino-The-children-despise-their-parents-until-the-age-of-when-they-suddenly.

"Quote by Robert Green Ingersoll." n.d. Quotes.Net. Accessed February 26, 2020. https://www.quotes.net/quote/14418.

"Thank You, Lord by Seth and Bessie Sykes."
n.d. HymnPod. Accessed February 25, 2020. http://
hymnpod.com/2009/01/27/thank-you-lord/.

"The Healer by Lois Irwin, 1955." n.d. Hymnary.Org.
Accessed February 26, 2020. https://hymnary.org/text/
on_the_cross_crucified_in_great_sorrow_h.

The Holy Bible: King James Version [KJV]. 1999. New
York, NY: American Bible Society. Public Domain.

The Holy Bible: New International Version [NIV].
1984. Grand Rapids: Zonderman Publishing
House. https://www.biblegateway.com/versions/
New-International-Version-NIV-Bible/#booklist.

The Holy Bible: New Living Translation [NLT]. n.d.
Carol Stream: Tyndale House Foundation. Tyndale
House Publishers, Inc. https://www.biblegateway.com/
versions/New-Living-Translation-NLT-Bible/#booklist.

*The Holy Bible: The New King James Version
[NKJV]*. 1999. Nashville, TN: Thomas Nelson,
Inc. https://www.biblegateway.com/versions/
New-King-James-Version-NKJV-Bible/#booklist.

"The Love of God by Frederick M. Lehman, 1917." n.d. Hymnary.Org. Accessed February 26, 2020. https://hymnary.org/text/the_love_of_god_is_greater_far.

"The Rainy Day by Henry Wadsworth Longfellow -." n.d. All Poetry. Accessed February 26, 2020. https://allpoetry.com/the-rainy-day.

"The Road Not Taken by Robert Frost." n.d. Academy of American Poets. Accessed February 26, 2020. https://poets.org/poem/road-not-taken.

"To God Be the Glory by Fanny Crosby, 1875." n.d. Hymnary.Org. Accessed February 25, 2020. https://hymnary.org/text/to_god_be_the_glory_great_things_he_hath.

"To God Be the Glory by Fanny Crosby, 1975." n.d. Hymnary.Org. Accessed February 25, 2020. https://hymnary.org/text/to_god_be_the_glory_great_things_he_hath.

Tranmer, Ron. n.d. "Broken Chain by Ron Tranmer." RonTranmer.Com. Accessed February

25, 2020. https://www.rontranmer.com/broken-chain-original/.

"Wonderful, Jesus Is to Me by Haldor Lillenas, 1924." 2020. Mobile Hymns. 2020. http://mobilehymns.org/english/Wonderful_Jesus_Is_To_Me.html.

"Wonderful Grace of Jesus by Haldor Lillenas, 1918." n.d. Hymnary.Org. Accessed February 26, 2020. https://hymnary.org/text/wonderful_grace_of_jesus.

"You Are My King by Billy James Foote, 2001." n.d. Wikipedia, The Free Encyclopedia. Accessed March 29, 2020. https://en.wikipedia.org/wiki/You_Are_My_King_(Amazing_Love).

"You Are My Sunshine – Original by Jimmie Davis 1940." n.d. Daisylinden.Com. Accessed February 26, 2020. https://daisylinden.com/you-are-my-sunshine-lyrics/.

About the Author

My name is Naomi Jean Radle.

CPSIA information can be obtained
at www.ICGtesting.com
Printed in the USA
LVHW022035270720
661655LV00013B/1414